EXPECTED DATE OF DEPARTURE

Preparing for the Death of Loved Ones

OLUBUSOLA (BUSOLA) ESHIET

OCL - Optimal Books

Expected Date of Departure
Preparing for the Death of Loved Ones

Olubusola (Busola) Eshiet

OCL - Optimal Books
Expected Date of Departure
Preparing for the Death of Loved Ones
© 2020 by Olubusola Eshiet
All rights reserved
Published by
OCL - Optimal Books, A division of Optimalpath Consulting Limited

Requests for permission to quote from this book should be directed to:
The Permission Unit, Optimal Books, Optimalpath Consulting Limited, The
Beacon, Westgate Road, Newcastle Upon Tyne, NE4 9PQ, United Kingdom,
or contact us via email at info@optimalpathconsulting.co.uk

Real names of people have been used in many instances, but some names
have been changed.

Unless otherwise stated, all Scripture quotations are from The Holy Bible,
New International Version Copyright ©1973, 1978, 1984 by International
Bible Society

CONTENTS

For Emmanuel
You let me talk to you about death
as much as I do about life
You add much beauty to my life.

PRAISE FOR OLUBUSOLA (BUSOLA) ESHIET

Thank you for being vulnerable and opening your heart in this way. Your book has touched on sensitive places in my heart; reading it has made me come face-to-face with my fear of losing my loved ones – to challenge that fear and begin my healing journey. I know that it will do the same for others.
   ChiChi Nwosu, Sydney, Australia

Everyone goes through the same problem of fear of bereavement, but no one wants to verbalise it. Many people are walking around afraid but don't want to say, "I'm feeling this way, how can I overcome it?" I must commend her for her ability to capture in words those feelings that a lot of people who have experienced loss find difficult to explain.
   Sunday Udo, Abidjan, Cote d'Ivoire

An unusual slant to an everyday reality. It is still a hard reality for me to face; but face it we must. Thankfully, God gave the answers to the puzzle long before the puzzle. Yes, we mourn the loss of loved ones but we are not driven to despair, knowing that we will meet again.
   This book inspires us to take steps to appreciate the people in our lives every day.
   Thank you Busola, for this push to prepare for the inevitable.
   Abimbola Olufemi, Lagos, Nigeria

Captivating, needful and relatable. Expected Date of Departure *is a must read for everyone as we all will depart this world at some point. It could happen sooner or later, but it is the only certain fact of life. While we all know this, most of us do not prepare for the departure of our loved ones if they pre-decease us. Olubusola has written a* book which gives practical tips on how to prepare, using real life experiences of friends and family and her own experience of losing loved ones. The book discusses the difficult issue of death in a way that the subject does not come across as morbid. Instead, it encourages us to break the silence surrounding the issue no one wants to talk about with sensitivity, understanding and empathy. Based on the word of God, it is encouraging and comforting. It is a book that is relatable as almost everyone has experienced the pain of losing a loved one. I highly recommend that everyone gets a copy and reads it.

Ibiba Chidi, Houston, Texas

This book is brilliant. It made me laugh and cry, it left me pondering many a question. Very important issues raised, and I love how much of the Word that Busola has included. Really well written. In my head it was just like she was talking to me as I read. Busola has put a lot of herself into this book and I pray that it helps many.

Sarah McManus, Newcastle upon Tyne, UK

I like Busola's boldness in confronting this matter. It's a subject that Nigerians, even Christians, avoid, with the crisp phrase 'not my portion'. Grief is heightened when one is totally unaware of what to expect in bereavement. Preparation will help people to set their relationships in order.

I appreciate Busola's courage in taking this discussion head-on.

Ijeoma Okafor John- Chieme, Abuja, Nigeria

As much as we tend to discount this truth, death is an inevitable part of life. Expected Date of Departure reminds me that life is a gift. I should be prepared, with peace in my heart, for the end of my life here on earth and let go of my loved ones when it's their time.

I find this book to be a valuable cross-cultural resource for starting conversations around the subjects of life and death. It is rich with personal experiences and spiritual insights. Busola, thank you for *writing this book. It gave me the rare luxury to pause and shed a few private tears in loving memory of my dear parents. My take-away from this book is to be more intentional in finding opportunities to enjoy the blessing of time with loved ones.*

Semedeton Ilo, Lethbridge, Canada

ACKNOWLEDGMENTS

I am grateful to everyone who has helped me in making the writing of this book possible.

My friends who read the draft and told me it's relevant and made suggestions and prayed.

Everyone who responded to my prodding questions and shared their pain to bless others, and Ijeoma who not only shared but gave her time to read the draft and provide useful feedback.

All who have written on the subject before me, whose words I quoted.

Alison, for many hours of meeting and proofreading; sharing her personal experience and providing a sounding board and to the Bowie Clan for their support.

Ebere, for the many miles she walked with me in Newcastle talking and praying through the ideas of the book, reading with me, and challenging the content. We came through!

Ihechi and Ihuoma who faithfully reminded me for two years that I meant to write this book.

Emmanuel for releasing me in many more ways that I can

recount to write and for listening again even when he heard me share an idea a hundred times.

All my amazing ever-loving siblings for reading all or part of the drafts and confirming that the family stories are accurate.

I give all the glory and honour to God the giver of ideas and provider of grace for enabling me to write this book.

FOREWORD

When our loved ones die, we suffer loss. Our lives will go on, but we will live with the knowledge that we will never be together in the same space with them again on this side of life. This is certain. Yet this certainty is not treated with the seriousness it deserves. Most people hardly discuss it; hardly plan for it and hardly learn any coping skills. Even when they mention death, it is usually done in hushed tones as you would a taboo. The discussion is often limited to when death has occurred. But should we prepare for bereavement or should we continue to avoid discussing it?

Busola answers this and other questions in her profound, faith-propelled book, *Expected Date of Departure: Preparing for the Death of Loved Ones*. In this book, you will find coping strategies based on deep faith, personal experience, research, and concern for people.

Busola has challenged us to think deeply and to remove the taboo associated with thinking, talking, and planning for death

Don't imagine that this is a grim book. It is, in fact, remarkably passionate, empathetic, and practical, all attributes of the author. I should know; Busola is my friend 'like-a-sister'.

For nearly thirty years, I have known her as a 'Daughter of Encouragement'. Busola is not theorising on what should be done; she supports the bereaved and has lived the experience of loss and grief. She finds fulfilment in reaching out to people who hurt, placing a comforting hand on their shoulder, a hug around them and words of encouragement in their hearts. She goes a step beyond to offer practical help when those people have been too weak, too distraught to think of any rational action. The testimonies abound in the book. So, I am not surprised that she would articulate these in one resource to help a wider spectrum of people beyond her friendship and family circle.

I may be biased, but I know you will not want to drop this captivating book until you have read through it. You would want to keep it as a self-help manual and for others around you. You will get the help you need to cope with your loss and discover how other people have coped. You will be ready to have that conversation with your loved ones about your own death and theirs, and you will find hope in God's ability to comfort you when you lose someone. You will realise that you are not alone but one of many who are asking questions about death, maybe in hushed tones. Now you are freed to bring the discussion to the open table.

Ebere Nweze

PROLOGUE: GOD FORBID!

Questions tug at my mind
But dare I ask!
Such questions aren't asked
You bury them in your heart
Let no one know I have such questions
But answers come only by asking
Perhaps I should ask?
Perhaps others want to ask
But who will bell the cat?
- *Olubusola Eshiet*

The one who asks questions doesn't lose his way[1]

In the early 90s, I walked into a Christian bookshop and my eyes caught a book *Early Widow*. I felt drawn to the book and decided to buy it. I can't forget the bewilderment on the faces of the two young ladies at the payment point; they couldn't come to terms with why I would buy such a book. I did not look like I was a widow (not that widows have a set look), and I was not. They asked me almost simultaneously, 'do you want to give it to a widow as a present?' I said, 'No, I want to read it'. And they asked me why I would want to read the book. You wouldn't understand their shock and their persuasion that I should not buy the book until you know that I was born and raised in a culture where we say 'God forbid' or 'it's not my portion' when there is a mention of anything that sounds like a misfortune. In addition, Christians were taught to confess positive things and not think of anything 'evil' befalling them. As a common example, when one felt tired or unwell, we weren't to say, 'I feel weak'; rather, we would say, 'I am strong'.

Anyhow, I succeeded in persuading the ladies to let me pay for the book. I read the book mostly in secret because just as I had to answer questions from the checkout staff, I would've had to answer even more questions from my friends and family if anyone found me reading the book.

So, it was no surprise that when a good friend of mine found me reading the book, she was alarmed at my morbid perception of life! Her face was aghast when she asked me, 'What's the problem?' She didn't ask if there was a problem because there MUST be a problem for me to be reading such a book at that point in my life. She tried to talk me out of reading it and wondered why I was so pessimistic about life. You shouldn't blame her.

You see, I was a young woman; I was approaching my twenty ninth birthday. I had a great relationship with my husband and two wonderful children then. I was the oldest of seven children and my siblings all adored me and looked up to me for guidance in different aspects of their lives. I adored them too and we were all fond of one another. I had healthy parents, a wonderful church family and a great circle of friends. I was in a season of learning new things and enjoying all my blessings. I wasn't sick, depressed, nor struggling in my relationships with God or with the people around me. My husband, children and siblings were in good health. My life was perfect.

My friend couldn't see any reason why I should be reading a book about widowhood; 'does the Bible not say that God will satisfy us with long life? Your husband is healthy. Many people will readily exchange their lives for what you have and here you are buying and reading a book about widowhood'. Those were my friend's words. You shouldn't blame her for being alarmed, nor should I!

My friend was not the only one who thought it was odd that I should be reading such a book. One of my sisters recently sent me a piece that she titled 'Confession'.

In 1992, after my secondary school, I came to live with you. I saw you reading the book *Early Widow* and I thought to myself 'why on earth will a young woman be reading this book? Is she preparing for the early death of her husband? I just didn't understand you!'

Another sister offered:

When my husband visited you at your home decades ago, he asked me 'why does sister have a book on widowhood on her bookshelf?' And I responded, 'that's just my sister.'

Obviously, I didn't do a good job of hiding the book. I

can't help wondering how many other people I caused to be alarmed whilst I thought I read my book in hiding!

OUR PERCEPTION OF LIFE

Our world tends to be preoccupied with life in the now whilst avoiding anything that remotely suggests pain or death. Science is racing to find ways to prolong life or to freeze ageing. Plastic surgery and make-over centres abound. More medications are prescribed to reduce pain, reduce disease, and promote a state of vivacious living, all welcome developments. The problem is that when things don't go well, the world blames God.

The Church seems to have been influenced by the world around her, so the Church isn't left out of this chase for zest here and now. Christians want to prosper; rightly so! We want God to prolong our lives; we want many blessings. And though it is right to ask God for what we desire, do we leave the choice of how to answer our prayers to God? We do believe that God is good all the time and we sing about it but we tend to decide what is good and we choose to miss out on Romans 8:28 'all things work together for our good'. When we insist on telling God how to answer our prayers, we may find ourselves blaming the devil for everything we perceive as negative. So, whilst the world blames God for everything perceived as negative that happens around us, the Christian blames the devil. It is a blame game, whichever way one looks at it. Perhaps the church needs to do more teaching on 'the fellowship of His suffering' (Philippians 3:10), and 'taking up our cross to follow him' (Matthew 16:24-26). Teachings in this area may be just as necessary as teachings on blessings, abundance and happiness. It is important that older Christians let new believers know that receiving Christ does not shield us from the trials that other people around us experience. The difference is that when we come to Christ, God gives us the grace that we require to face those trials. As Yvonne Richmond Tulloch says, we need to watch out against triumphalism and to remember that before Easter, there was the pain of Good Friday and the confusion of Easter Saturday. All the days together make Easter.[1] Jesus bore the physical pain of crucifixion, the emotional pain of betrayal, denial and wrong accusation, not to mention that his friends and disciples felt disappointed and abandoned. All these events preceded the triumph of his resurrection. A trial usually comes before a victory.

Let me take you back to my friend. As I mentioned, death is never discussed in advance by young people in the culture that I was raised. That discussion is for older people, maybe those in their 60s and older. People are discouraged from discussing death as it is assumed that discussing or preparing for death is an ominous sign and talking about it may even send an invitation to bad luck, including death itself. Even when someone is sick and has been given a terminal diagnosis, discussing the person's death or what will happen to the dependants and loved ones afterwards is not encouraged. Also, when the person has been told they have just a few months or weeks to live, if you start discussing the possibility of the person's death, the interpretation is that you wish the person dead. You could be accused of killing the person by witchcraft if they eventually died.

In fact, most people prepare for everything about their lives and relationships and they have a set schedule for specific events to do for and with their family and friends but very few prepare for anything about the death of loved ones; they do not allow themselves to think about it. Many refuse to even write a will. Discussing one's life after the death of one's spouse with the spouse is almost tantamount to wishing that the spouse is dead! You now know more reasons for my friend's alarm.

No 'normal' or 'reasonable' person would add a book about grief and mourning to their book purchases or reading list unless they are in the middle of a grief situation. Even in this state, many sympathisers would encourage the grieving person to read books that would cheer them up, books that would help them forget and not those that could add to their depression and gloom. Why should they compound their problems by reading such negative reminders?

So why would I buy a book about widowhood and grief?

To answer this question, it might be helpful for you to know that I have lost family members (my brother during my childhood, my grandmother who raised me and was the first mother I really knew, another brother, and my nephew); I have lost close friends. Moreover, I have friends who have lost spouses (more have lost spouses after the time I bought the book), children, siblings and parents. Many dear Christian brothers and sisters have died at various points in my Christian walk. In all these losses, I have found myself deeply immersed in grief whether I was the one bereaved, or I was supporting someone who was bereaved.

I was unconsciously drawn to the book because I wanted to understand how people survived such losses. How does someone feel when they are told their husband has died? What would the person do and how do they ever survive such a heartbreak? Since I bought that first book on grief, I've read many others as I sought comfort in the stories of others who have suffered the loss of loved ones. In reading these books, I sought answers to those questions and many others that rang in my mind that I wasn't able to articulate or dare discuss with anyone without their wondering if I was of a sound mind. I'm sure that if I had dared share my musings with my friend at the time, I would have caused her more alarm. Some of the questions may have given those around me cause to worry and ask that deliverance prayers be offered on my behalf to chase the combination of melancholic thinking and morbidity out of me. I didn't want either to happen. I knew that I didn't need to have demons chased out of me instead I needed answers to my questions.

So how have I handled grieving when confronted with the death of loved ones? In the past, I griped and grieved hard when I suffered a loss or when people around me suffered. I usually felt palpable pains, a throbbing disconnect and internal chaos that bordered on panic. I lost sleep too. No, I didn't question God nor momentarily lose my faith in Him. I have always revered God as unquestionable and I was sure He had His good plans. I love heaven and look forward to going there, but that did not change anything about my discontent with parting with loved ones. Why would I feel affected by loss in this way? I wished I didn't have to be so broken and didn't have to grieve with such intensity.

Nearly three decades later, and after reading many more such books on bereavement and mourning, I'm still asking these questions, but I'm getting bolder with my investigation. I'm no longer afraid to ask them of people around me nor indeed to bring the discussion to the public square. This is one reason I have chosen to write this book. I intend to examine and discuss my personal experience and those of other Christians in grief, and Christian writings about grief and mourning. In addition, I will be looking out for experiences that differ from what I have been used to in myself and others, and what I have read and listened to about grieving.

My questions are:

1. Is there any exception to grieving in the way we are accustomed?
2. Are there people whose grieving patterns do not

conform to the stages of grief that I have experienced, heard, or read about? In other words, are there people who have felt a sense of comfort that has lasted beyond the period of shock and denial and who moved forward with their grief without having the typical experiences of pain, or are these just impossible wishes?

3. Is there anyone that has been known to have suffered the loss of a precious one and did not experience these agonising pangs of grief?

4. Is there a way I could be shielded from such pains when I undergo loss?

5. Is it not possible that God cuts off the immediate and chaotic pain that follows loss and helps one gather oneself together from the onset or even fast track the known process of grief?

6. Are there people who have had such experiences and would be willing to share?

I could go on and on with questions. These questions simply express my wishes; wishes that I could face grief with confidence and strength when I first receive the unpleasant news of the death of a loved one and that I will be able to keep processing my grief with strength and confidence, and maybe, much less pain than can be imagined.

In this book I invite you to join me on a journey of reflection and possible discovery. I hope you will find this book helpful for whatever loss you are facing right now and a preparation for those you will face in the future. I hope you will find comfort that will help you to comfort others (2 Corinthians 1:4).

I embarked on the writing of this book in the hope of finding some answers. I don't claim to have found many, but I hope together, we will make some valuable discoveries. For this to be a shared journey, may I invite you to take a few moments and answer some Grief Readiness questions below? You will be asked to repeat it at the end of the book.

The questions aim to find out your readiness to talk about death and willingness to prepare your mind for the possible death of loved ones of any age.

1. In what specific ways do you miss someone you love when you have to part from them for a relatively long time (e.g. travel, relocation, etc.)?
2. What things do you think you will miss about your loved ones if they should die before you do (please state relationships)?
3. What makes the relationships with your loved ones special to you?
4. What are your immediate thoughts/feelings on thinking they may die before you?
5. Do you talk to your loved ones about their death and your death? If so, what triggered these conversations?
6. Imagine you hear that they have died, how does this make you feel?
7. How will you cope with the grief of losing them?
8. What regrets would you have if they died suddenly?
9. Are there activities that you can engage in now that will make your loss more bearable, e.g. how to do things around the home, places to go, or general information?

Should I come that close to you
Or even allow you come this close to me
It's good to be close, Oh, how warm
But is it right to be close
Seeing we can be separated
Without even a moment's notice
Or should we keep a distance
So parting will not be that hard?
- *Olubusola Eshiet*

Grief is the price we pay for love.[1]

FEAR OF LOSS

I can say with a certainty that I'm not afraid to die. In God's appointed time, I will die. Call it a relocation – sure. I know I'll change address from my earthly body and physical home to my spiritual body and live in heaven eternally with my Saviour and Lord, Jesus Christ. Jesus has freed me from slavery of fear of death – fear of dying.

From earliest childhood recollections, I've been homesick for heaven. My favourite songs have been those which speak of heaven, heavenly Jerusalem, our last home that Christ has gone to prepare for us. One of them is *Jerusalem on High* which I first learnt in my mother tongue (Yoruba): *Jerusalem t'orun*. Others include *I love my Jesus* (by Evie Karlsson), and the more recent *10,000 Reasons* (by Matt Redman).

Although songs about heaven remain my most loved songs and I look forward to seeing my Saviour, Lord, King and Friend, and just kneel at His feet to say how much I love Him, I must admit that for much of my adult life I have had a persistent fear of death; not the fear of *my* dying but the fear of my loved ones dying. It is the fear of loss of loved ones.

I've wondered why God would give us people to love and

then choose to take them in His own time. Why this loan, though interest-free, when we must lose them after we become so attached to them? I think on the song: *Remind Me Dear Lord*; the writer rightly says that God should remind us that the things we cling to and love much are not ours but borrowed.

But why can't we be together for ever? I don't mind returning loans of material possessions, but of human beings, husband, child, friend, parents, No! No! No! Can you hear my cries? Straight from my heart. Can't I keep them for ever?

Oh, I've always wanted to be with God, the saints and angels in heaven. But that doesn't change anything! I know for sure we'll meet again in heaven, but I longed that I didn't have to let go of anyone I love on this earth. I mean, they're irreplaceable, the gap they leave can't be filled. I no longer feel the pain of loss when I think of my grandmother, but I still miss her. Could my brother not have regained his health and lived (I'm writing this 39 year after he died). I think of my nephew and the words in my head remain, 'he was such a good one; he should have lived'.

Thoughts of my loved ones dying seem to be a constant companion. The thoughts just come, uninvited. I seem unable to stop them. Have you ever wished you didn't have certain thoughts, yet they keep flying into your mind in a way that seems as if they need no permission to do so? They came as frequently as they wanted, and those thoughts filled my heart with fear.

Will I see my parents alive again? I inwardly groan at the thought of not seeing them again especially as I live far away from them and can't make a quick dash to see them if I ever needed to.

Will my child survive this sickness (when they were younger)?

What if my husband does not come back from the current trip, what if the plane or car crashes, what if any of the misfortunes that can befall a tourist happens to him, or what if he even gets attacked while tending the garden just outside the house?

Will this be the last time I will see my friend? Will s/he survive this illness? Will my siblings/friends/ extended family members all survive the Corona Virus (happening as I write)?

The above and more are questions that pop into my mind regularly, maybe a bit more frequently than I would like them to. Like it or not, they come to my mind and they insist on answers. I didn't and still don't have answers to these questions. I didn't know if I would see my parents alive again neither did I know for certain that my children would outlive all the illnesses. Thank God they did.

I've heard a few variations of this saying credited to Martin Luther:

> You cannot stop a bird from flying over your head but what you can do is stop it from perching on your head and building a nest there.

I can't stop the thoughts from popping up in my mind at the most unexpected moments, but I can decide whether to welcome them with a 'fear party' or to show them the way out. I think that in my earlier days of facing these thoughts, my response was more of fear and the kind of prayers I prayed back then were what someone described as 'feverish prayers'. My understanding of feverish prayers are ones that are not based on confidence in the Word of God but are in response to anxieties. I would quote all the Bible verses that speak about God's protection and long life, but I would still be fearful. I didn't give up on praying though, I couldn't give up. I kept holding on to the Word of God to save me from the fear that accompanied those thoughts. I don't remember when, but I began to have another set of questions:

1. What does God say to me about fear?
2. Has Christ's death made any provision for my situation – fear of death of loved ones?

These set of questions are different from the earlier ones because I know I can find answers to them in the Bible.

1. To the first question 'what does God say to me about fear?', I have this answer: *For God has not given us a spirit of fear, but of power and of love and of a sound mind.* 2 Timothy 1:7 (KJV).
2. To the second question 'has Christ's death made any provision for my situation – fear of death of loved ones?', I have this answer: *Since the children have flesh and blood, he too shared in their humanity so that by his death he might destroy him who holds the power of death - that is, the devil and free those who all their lives were held in slavery by their fear of death.* Hebrews 2:14-15

Finding these answers set me on the path to deliverance and helped to provide me with the right answers to the previous questions. I now have knowledge. Hosea 4:6 says: *"My people are destroyed from lack of knowledge".* The knowledge of the truth drives away fear. This doesn't refer to merely knowing what the Bible says but believing it and acting with a conviction that it is the truth. Hence Jesus said: *If you hold to my teaching, you are really my disciples. Then you will know the truth, and the truth will set you free.* John 8: 31-32.

All fear is fear. If I am afraid of my loved ones dying, it simply means that I am afraid. Who has given me the spirit of fear? Not God, the giver of all good and perfect gifts (James 1:17).

Our God is in the gift giving business, but one thing he will never tie a bow on to give to you is fear.[1]

I agree completely with this. So, being sure that fear is not from God, I reject the fear of loss each time it comes, and I embrace the gift of God, a sound mind. By answering this question, I can reject the agony that comes with fear of losing loved ones. For indeed, 'fear involves torment' (1 John 4:18, NKJV).

In answering the second question, 'has Christ's death made any provision for my situation – fear of death of loved ones?', I acknowledged that I should make full use of the provision made by Christ's death to free me from the slavery to the fear of death, even the death of others. As a result, I can walk in the liberty that Christ has given me. And then I realised that both questions address the same root – fear. When I deal with the fear of loss of loved ones, I can pray for them with confidence in the promises of protection God has given in the Bible. I can truly and fully place my loved ones in God's protective care and be at peace. When those questions that used to make me afraid come, I answer honestly that I don't know about the 'ifs' but I know for sure that God is able to keep all that I have put in His care and this includes myself and my loved ones (2 Tim 1:10-12). This knowledge means I don't have to be afraid for them or for myself. God is able to keep us all. I cannot describe what peace this knowledge brings. And where else is there such reassurance as there is in the Bible?

GOD'S WORD ON LOSS

All over the Bible, especially in the Psalms and the book of Job, there are words of comfort and encouragement in the midst of mourning. This is not surprising as these two men

(David and Job) are models in the study on suffering, sorrow, mourning, words of laments and at the same time, dependence on God for comfort. Job may be described as a person who suffered the greatest loss imaginable in all times. It is doubtful that someone would be found who lost everything in one day as Job did. If there was a Hall of Fame of Loss, he would likely be the most qualified member! Job's experience of crushing was so deep that no-one would invite such an experience if given the choice.

Who is to Blame?

Job lost his seven children and all his wealth in one day and soon after, he started to lose his health, and the support of his wife too! If you don't already know the end of the story, you may now be wondering what Job's sin was and why he deserved to be punished so severely. Often, when tragedy befalls us or someone we know, we may find ourselves playing the blame game. We and other people (even Christians) around us try to suggest that our suffering is a result of our bad choice, or of what we or someone else did or did not do. Job's friends were no different. To be fair, they sat with him in silence for days, certainly a commendable act. Many people fail to understand the need of the bereaved person for less chatter and more silent support. However, with the passage of time, even Job's friends suggested strongly that Job must have sinned, or if he did not sin, his children must have sinned. Eliphaz subtly implied that innocent people do not perish nor are the upright ever destroyed (Job 4:7-8). Bildad was more direct in stating that Job's children sinned against God (Job 8:4). We may have experienced being blamed when bad things happen to us, and maybe we play the role of self-accusation. For some reason, it appears that there is some temporary sense of relief in self-blame or in blaming someone else when calamity calls. However, the Bible makes it clear that Job loved and obeyed God; he was blameless and upright (Job 1:1&8). It was not Job's fault nor the fault of his children. There was no-one to blame. It seems that life just happened. A closer look at Job 1 and 2 gives a more detailed account.

The Bible presents some interesting examples of people who died or were spared death under circumstances that look similar. Peter and James, disciples of Jesus were each arrested for being disciples and the penalty chosen by their accusers was death. James was killed but God sent an angel to release Peter. Can anyone find something to blame James or the other disciples for? Is there anything Peter did better or was he better supported by the other disciples? Did they pray more, or have more faith? Why did their similar situations produce different outcomes? There was no evidence of Peter praying all night; he was sleeping when the angel came for him (Acts 12: 6-7); nor of him demonstrating greater faith than James. The disciples who were praying earnestly for Peter were caught off guard by his release. When Rhoda who answered the doorbell for Peter told the praying disciples that it was Peter at the door, the same disciples who were praying earnestly for him told Rhoda that she was halluci-nating and concluded that she must have seen 'Peter's angel' (Acts 12: 15-16). A third example is Stephen who was arrested for the same reason, preaching the good news that Jesus was the Messiah, the expected Son of God.

Now Stephen, a man full of God's grace and power, performed great wonders and signs among the people. Acts 6:8

However, Stephen was not spared but stoned to death. Can anyone think of passing some blame here? Did Stephen need more faith? Did he say the wrong thing? Did he sin against God? Was he in the right place at the wrong time and so did he miss God's timing? I doubt anyone will answer 'yes' to any of these questions.

Why then do we seek to find who is to blame when someone we love dies? People blame God, satan, themselves, or the dead person. When we think a death is untimely, we say: 'If only I had told her not to go'; 'if he had listened to me'; 'if she had listened to the Holy Spirit, she would not have been on that flight'; 'it must be because he spoke rudely to the pastor, does the Bible not say to do the prophet of God no harm'; and on and on.

Job did not blame himself, nor did he accept his friends' attempt to blame him for the tragedies that befell him. We could learn a lesson from Job. It is sad enough to have to mourn a loved one; why should anyone add the extra burden of blame to this? While Job was in grief, he directed his heartache and anguished questions in surrender to God. His immediate response is legendary:

> *The Lord gave and the Lord has taken away; may the name of the Lord be praised. Job 1:20*

Why?

Perhaps another burden people carry is the 'why' question: 'If only I could know why this happened'. I wish I could put this in a milder way, but may it be simpler to understand if we just agree that the first and easiest answer to the question as to why someone has died is that people will inevitably die. That is the point of this book: everyone will die; it is only a matter of when. So, our first point of preparation may be to accept that everyone will die at some point and we will live to mourn friends and family, if we haven't already begun to do so.

> *Your eyes saw my unformed body; all the days*

ordained for me were written in your book before one of them came to be. Psalm 139:16

Before I formed you in the womb, I knew you, and before you were born, I set you apart and appointed you a prophet to the nations. Jeremiah 1:5

*There is a time for everything, and a season for every activity under the heavens: **a time to be born and a time to die**. Ecclesiastes 3:1-2 (Emphasis mine)*

Although this reason may appear an insufficient answer, it may be helpful to start with it. But this brings many other questions:

Why now, and not later, as desired?

Why should I then pray for healing for my sick and dying loved ones? Why not resign and accept that it will happen?

These are good questions to ask as we seek the balance between the determination to see God work in healing us and our loved ones and the acceptance of God's sovereignty.

To answer these questions, I will turn to the Bible again and to the experiences of Christians who have shared their application of God's words to their situations as they prayed for themselves or sick and dying loved ones and even for protection over loved ones who are not sick or in any obvious danger.

In those days Hezekiah became ill and was at the point of death. The prophet Isaiah son of Amoz went to him and said, "This is what the Lord says: Put your house in order, because you are going to die; you will not recover."

> *Hezekiah turned his face to the wall and prayed to*
> *the Lord, "Remember, Lord, how I have walked*
> *before you faithfully and with wholehearted*
> *devotion and have done what is good in your*
> *eyes." And Hezekiah wept bitterly.*
> *Before Isaiah had left the middle court, the word of*
> *the Lord came to him: "Go back and tell*
> *Hezekiah, the ruler of my people, 'This is what*
> *the Lord, the God of your father David, says: I*
> *have heard your prayer and seen your tears; I will*
> *heal you. On the third day from now you will go*
> *up to the temple of the Lord. I will add fifteen*
> *years to your life. And I will deliver you and this*
> *city from the hand of the king of Assyria. I will*
> *defend this city for my sake and for the sake of my*
> *servant David.'"*
> *Then Isaiah said, "Prepare a poultice of figs." They*
> *did so and applied it to the boil, and he recovered.*
> *2 Kings 20: 1-7*

Hezekiah's story shows the desirable 'ask and you will receive' situation. He prayed to God and God gave him fifteen more years. This is the kind of answer that I would be happy to receive from God. Hezekiah reminded God that he had walked faithfully with God. However, there was another man, Moses, who had walked faithfully with God. In addition to all that we know of Moses' faithfulness and diligence in carrying out God's instruction, it was said about him:

> *(Now Moses was a very humble man, more humble*
> *than anyone else on the face of the earth.)*
> *Numbers 12:3*

In spite of this, we read about Moses:

At that time I pleaded with the Lord: "Sovereign Lord, you have begun to show to your servant your greatness and your strong hand. For what god is there in heaven or on earth who can do the deeds and mighty works you do? Let me go over and see the good land beyond the Jordan—that fine hill country and Lebanon."

But because of you the Lord was angry with me and would not listen to me. "That is enough," the Lord said. "Do not speak to me anymore about this matter. Go up to the top of Pisgah and look west and north and south and east. Look at the land with your own eyes, since you are not going to cross this Jordan."

Deuteronomy 3: 23-27

And in Deuteronomy 34: 1-7:

Then Moses climbed Mount Nebo from the plains of Moab to the top of Pisgah, across from Jericho. There the Lord showed him the whole land— from Gilead to Dan, all of Naphtali, the territory of Ephraim and Manasseh, all the land of Judah as far as the Mediterranean Sea, the Negev and the whole region from the Valley of Jericho, the City of Palms, as far as Zoar. Then the Lord said to him, "This is the land I promised on oath to Abraham, Isaac and Jacob when I said, 'I will give it to your descendants.' I have let you see it with your eyes, but you will not cross over into it."

And Moses the servant of the Lord died there in Moab, as the Lord had said. He buried him in Moab, in the valley opposite Beth Peor, but to this day no one knows where his grave is.

Moses was so special that God himself buried him and no one knows where his grave is. But he died. God didn't answer Moses' appeal for a longer life and for seeing the Promised Land. The same God, different responses to prayers. Taking Hezekiah and Moses' accounts as examples, we should do our part, which is to pray. The two men prayed earnestly; they made their appeal to God. We should pray as if we expect God to answer. If we don't pray, there will be no expectation of an answer and we may lose the opportunity of having our health or that of a loved one restored. We should ask with the full expectation to receive, and yes, pray that mountains of ill health be moved. All over the world, Christians are experiencing answers to their prayers. I have had my prayer answered and a long-standing ovarian cyst melted away in defiance of medical expectations. I had been advised that only surgery would remove the cyst and that wasn't strange to me. My family, friends, and I had trusted God for divine healing, but I had had two previous surgeries, 10 years apart, for the removal of ovarian cysts. Each time, I felt disappointed as I had hoped God would save me from the doctor's knife. However, when a cyst grew again, I went back to God in faith as before and this time, the cyst gradually melted away. I wish I could say that it was because I had more faith the last time than in the previous times, 'no'. Each time, I trusted God enough to go back to him. I prayed and expected to receive an answer each time and when I didn't receive the answer I wanted, I didn't allow that to discourage me from asking again.

I have often heard Christians say, 'God is God, and we are not'. We cannot lock God up and put the key in our pockets, He is sovereign. It is ours to ask, the answer should always be left to God. Even the Lord Jesus Christ asked the Father to take the cup of the suffering and crucifixion away from him.

> *Father, if you are willing, take this cup from me; yet*
> *not my will, **but yours be done**. Luke 22:42.*
> *(Emphasis mine)*

The difference between Jesus' prayer and mine used to be - and anyone else who prays like I did - is in the highlighted part. If we express our desire in faith and leave the decision to God, would we not be more at peace? In my earlier years as a Christian, I was taught that including 'if it is your will' in my prayer was a sign of doubt. I accepted this teaching and even now that I know that Jesus prayed to God in this manner, I still struggle with the reality of praying 'your will be done, Lord'. The struggle is not because I am afraid to pray for God's will, it is more a struggle with an old habit. I have learnt that whether we leave it to God or not, God will have his way.

Why then should we pray? The simple answer is we can only receive when we ask. If we don't ask, we won't receive.

> *Ask and it will be given to you; seek and you will*
> *find; knock and the door will be opened to you.*
> *Matthew 7:7.*

Tony Evans speaking on loss of his wife and other close family members and answering the question, 'if God is sovereign and his will is already determined, why do we pray?[2]', had this to say:

> God asked me "are you going to trust my heart when you don't understand my hand?"

God says I am only going to do this if you meet my requirements. Prayer is one of those requirements. You have not because you asked not. So, Paul says pray about all things.

We should do our part by praying as if we expect to be heard. If we don't pray, there will be no expectation of an answer and there will be nothing for God to answer.

But we should ask and leave to the sovereign Lord how to answer.

In Daniel chapter 3, we read that Shadrack, Meshach and Abednego told their persecutor, King Nebuchadnezzar, that their God (capital 'G')[3] was able to save them from the king's threat of killing them if they did not worship Nebuchadnezzar's god (small 'g'). They were certain that this was so, and they added that if God did not save them, not because he was unable but because he chose not to, they would still serve their God.

> *Shadrach, Meshach and Abednego replied to him,*
> *"King Nebuchadnezzar, we do not need to defend*
> *ourselves before you in this matter. If we are*
> *thrown into the blazing furnace, the God we*
> *serve is able to deliver us from it, and he will*
> *deliver us from Your Majesty's hand. But even if*
> *he does not, we want you to know, Your Majesty,*
> *that we will not serve your gods or worship the*
> *image of gold you have set up." Daniel 3:16-18*

So, when we pray, we should trust God for the best outcome. From my own experience, the outcome is almost always the same as I desire and so my life is filled with testimonies of answered prayers. But occasionally, no matter how much I pray, the outcome is different from what I hoped for. I do feel disappointed, just as Tony Evans said of himself in other parts of the interview quoted above but I choose to 'trust His heart instead of looking at His hand'. I remind myself of the uncountable answered prayers and I keep on trusting God for more. Jesus says we are to keep praying and never give up (Luke 18:1).

If you have had toothache or pain in your gums, you will agree with me that toothache or gum pain is an undesirable state of existence. For nearly five years, friends and family know that I have suffered from this condition and they have been praying with and for me. I have been in and out of the dentist's office. The pain has been known to stop me from having a good night's sleep and from attending a vital meeting. I keep praying and trusting God for healing because I know he heals and can heal me of any illness. I will not give up until I receive my healing.

Won't Let go

An aspect of asking relates to when God helps us to realise that the end has come for us or for someone we love. First, how do we know for sure that God is the one saying to us that the end has come? What if it is a whisper from the enemy, satan? Secondly, is it easy to accept this even when we are sure that God has spoken to us? Do we make use of such help to prepare ourselves for what we don't want but know may happen or do we fight against it until the last? Please note that I don't mean a resigned acceptance that death will come anyway so we don't pray. We must always have the faith that God can do all things and so can heal someone even at the last minute.

But just as we know the voice of God at other times, we can recognise his voice when he says it is time for this person to die, when he says: you should stop praying now and begin to accept that his/her time has come.

. . . and the sheep listen to his voice. He calls his own

17

> *sheep by name and leads them out. When he has*
> *brought out all his own, he goes on ahead of them,*
> *and his sheep follow him because they know his*
> *voice. But they will never follow a stranger; in*
> *fact, they will run away from him because they*
> *do not recognise a stranger's voice. John 10:3-5*

Sometimes, we do recognise his voice saying, it is time to let go but we are not willing to let go. It may be easier to let go of old people (age is relative) but of people we consider young, this may be difficult. A widow whose husband was terminally ill and who thought God had told her he would die said:

Does knowing that God has said this person will die make it any easier? NO. Acceptance is still a herculean task. There's a sense of fear and trepidation that fills you while waiting for the inevitable and a hope that this cup will pass away.

David was told clearly that the son that Bathsheba had for him would die but he fought for the life of his son till the child died.

> *But because by doing this you have shown utter*
> *contempt for the Lord, the son born to you will*
> *die."*
> *After Nathan had gone home, the Lord struck the*
> *child that Uriah's wife had borne to David, and*
> *he became ill. David pleaded with God for the*
> *child. He fasted and spent the nights lying in sack*
> *cloth on the ground. The elders of his household*
> *stood beside him to get him up from the ground,*
> *but he refused, and he would not eat any food*

with them. On the seventh day the child died. 2 Samuel 12:14-18

David fought for his son's life till the end. I don't blame him, and I would do the same, on the basis of 'Who knows? The Lord may be gracious to me and let the child live'. David understood the nature of God, His grace and therefore there was that very real possibility that God might relent. This was his child after all...

However, it appears David allowed the word of God to prepare him for the loss. To the surprise of his attendants, when the child died, David got up from the ground, cleaned himself up and asked for some food. Maybe we too will be able to act like David when we don't receive the desired outcome of our prayers for God to keep someone we love from dying.

> *His attendants asked him, "Why are you acting this way? While the child was alive, you fasted and wept, but now that the child is dead, you get up and eat!"*
> *He answered, "While the child was still alive, I fasted and wept. I thought, 'Who knows? The Lord may be gracious to me and let the child live.' But now that he is dead, why should I go on fasting? Can I bring him back again? I will go to him, but he will not return to me. 2 Samuel 12: 21-23*

In Bible, we read the story of a man who brought many people to know God, especially non-Jews and he had the opportunity to speak to kings and rulers about Jesus Christ. He healed uncountable people from sickness, and he raised the dead more than once. When a dangerous snake wrapped itself around his arm, he shook it off. God saved him from many attempts of people who hated him and wanted to kill him. Once, God caused his nephew to find out the plot by his enemies, so ending the plot (Acts 23:16-25). Another time, he was lowered in a basket over the fence of a city to make his escape Acts 9:25. This was the extent that God went to keep the man from harm. By now, it's highly likely that you know the man I'm describing here is Paul. He did many great miracles in the name of Jesus. I like Paul because not only did he know when God said 'no' but he was able to accept 'no' for an answer from God. He demonstrated this about a problem, which he said tormented him and that he wanted God to take away:

> Three times I pleaded with the Lord to take it away
> from me. But he said to me, "My grace is sufficient
> for you, for my power is made perfect in
> weakness. 2 Corinthians 12:8-9

For Paul, it was not a case of resigning to fate but of knowing that God has given him a decision about the matter. Also, when God told Paul he would be persecuted, put in chains and that he would not see certain friends again before he died (Acts 20:25; Acts21:10), he knew that was a decision God had made, not one to argue against or plead for a change but to work through, trusting God's heart and his ability to help Paul stand firm till the end. Paul knew the voice of God, we should also.

My friend Alison told me how she and her family prayed for a few months for healing for her mother from cancer. But at a point, she felt a clear leading from God that her role had changed from helping her mother to live to helping her mother die and preparing her father for the event. Painful as that knowledge was, she knew God had spoken to her and she no longer felt the release to pray for her mother's healing. She acted like Paul by staying close to her mother, providing all the support she could for her mother and for her father and she was there to sing hymns to her till she passed. I suppose Alison's mother would have died at that same time anyway, but mother and daughter would have lost all the wonderful opportunities of sharing those last weeks together in the way they did. Perhaps David too could have been spared a lot of heartache if he had accepted the decree of God sooner.

Another friend, Eby, told me that God helped her to realise during a visit to her father that this would the last time she and her family would see her father on this side of eternity. To be clear, Eby's father was in good health at the time. Knowing that she had heard from God, she made sure to conclude any unsettled business, especially discussing once more, the matter of his relationship with God and readiness to meet his maker. They prayed with him on the assurance of his salvation, and they had photographs together. That was truly the last time my friend saw her father. Three weeks later, her father died. If she hadn't accepted the prompting from God or had just prayed it off, she would have been left to regret and to wonder about her father's eternal fate.

It's interesting to note that in Paul's case above, he accepted that he wouldn't see his friends again but in some of the places, the friends didn't accept. They argued and even his close colleagues like Luke persuaded him not to go to Jerusalem. They were forced to accept that God's will be done when they couldn't stop Paul from going on the journey.

> *After we had been there a number of days, a prophet named Agabus came down from Judea. Coming over to us, he took Paul's belt, tied his own hands and feet with it and said, "The Holy Spirit says,*

> *'In this way the Jewish leaders in Jerusalem will*
> *bind the owner of this belt and will hand him*
> *over to the Gentiles.'"*
> *When we heard this,* **we *and the people there***
> ***pleaded with Paul not to go*** *up to*
> *Jerusalem. Then Paul answered, "Why are you*
> *weeping and breaking my heart? I am ready not*
> *only to be bound, but also to die in Jerusalem for*
> *the name of the Lord Jesus." When he would not*
> *be dissuaded, we gave up and said, "The Lord's*
> *will be done. Acts 21:10-14 (Emphasis mine)*

In very recent times, I was privileged to follow news about the declining health of a precious servant of God, Ravi Zacharias. I don't feel qualified to write about him as I only got to know about him shortly before he died. But I could see that he loved God and attracted many people to God. He travelled far and wide proclaiming the good news of salvation in Jesus and Jesus only. As his family informed his connections all over the world about the declining state of Ravi's physical body, I was fascinated by the terminology they used and the assurance that Ravi was about to go to his heavenly home. There was the sense of realisation by Ravi and his family that it was no longer the time to ask God to heal him but time to let go. Ravi had even requested that the casket to bear his body should come from a certain place. His loved ones had placed the order and it was reported as a thing of joy that the casket arrived in time, even before Ravi had breathed his last.[4] Depending on how you read this, you may think they should have had faith for Ravi's healing, whereas I thought it was a great way of responding in appreciation to God who gave them the opportunity to prepare for the departure and loss.

I would like to conclude this chapter with these two Bible passages:

> *For none of us lives for ourselves alone, and none of us dies for ourselves alone. If we live, we live for the Lord; and if we die, we die for the Lord. So, whether we live or die, we belong to the Lord. For this very reason, Christ died and returned to life so that he might be the Lord of both the dead and the living. Romans 14: 7-9*

> *Precious in the sight of the Lord is the death of his faithful servants. Psalm 116:15*

If I must do it
May I do it my way
It is unpleasant enough
So, may I be spared the additional burden
Of being instructed just how to do it
When now I barely know who I am
- *Olubusola Eshiet*

The Lord is close to the brokenhearted. He saves those whose spirits have been crushed. Psalm 34:18 (NRSV)

2: MOURNING MY WAY

Talking about Grief

Since we are considering the subject of loss, we must also consider grief because loss is always followed by grief.

I find much help in the definition:

Pentheo (translated as mourn)— '"to experience sadness or grief as the result of depressing circumstances or the condition of persons" – "to be sad, to grieve for, to weep for, sorrow, grief."' (2 Corinthians 12:21; Matt 5:4; James 4:9)[1]

Although I have seen definitions that attempt to differentiate between 'grieve' and 'mourn', these two words are often regarded as synonyms. In this chapter, the two words are interchangeable.

There is no one who can say they have never experienced sadness resulting from depressing circumstances. Susan Lenzkes, in her book, *Licking Honey Off A Thorn*, broadens the scope of things people grieve about to include everyday losses

and frustrations about life. We grieve the loss of lives, relationships, property, health, etc.

There is enough evidence to show that grieving the death
of a loved one is a matter of *when* not *if*. It will happen to
everyone although to some more times than to others.

The Bible is replete with examples of people grieving
from the Old to the New Testament. In addition to Job and
David already mentioned earlier, who were only a smattering
of the examples of people who grieved in the Old Testament,
the New Testament also shows examples of people who
grieved. These include Mary, Martha and Jesus. God-fearing
men grieved for Stephen (Acts 8:2), and believers mourned
Dorcas (Acts 9:36-42)). There is advice in the Bible on how to
grieve and a word about how not to grieve.

In addition, many people have written about their
personal experience of grief and those of others they have
encountered, supported, or counselled.

When Jesus' friend, Lazarus died, Jesus went to Bethany
and was met by Martha, Lazarus' sister who longed that Jesus
had been around. She knew her brother would not have died
for surely; Jesus would have healed his friend. When Mary,
the other sister of Lazarus came out, she expressed the same
thought:

> *When Mary reached the place where Jesus was and
> saw him, she fell at his feet and said, "Lord, if you
> had been here, my brother would not have died."*
> *John 11:32*

When Jesus saw her weeping, and the Jews who had come
along with her also weeping, he was deeply moved in spirit
and troubled. "Where have you laid him?" he asked.

> *"Come and see, Lord," they replied.* **Jesus wept**.

*Then the Jews said, "See how he loved him!" John
12:32-36 (Emphasis mine)*

Jesus who had taught his followers in Matthew 5:4,
'Blessed are those who mourn for they will be comforted'
showed by example that it is okay to mourn.

The Apostle Paul, writing to the Thessalonians said:

> *Brothers and sisters, we do not want you to be
> uninformed about those who sleep in death, so
> that you do not grieve like the rest of mankind,
> who have no hope. For we believe that Jesus died
> and rose again, and so we believe that God will
> bring with Jesus those who have fallen asleep in
> him. 1 Thessalonians 4:13-14*

The advice here is that although believers grieve, they
should not give room to hopelessness, or to thinking they will
never see their loved one again. Rather, they should take
comfort in knowing that Jesus will bring a restoration of relationships now temporarily broken by death. In other words,
though the parting is painful and will be for a while, we
should mourn like people who know that we will meet again.

REVIEW OF BOOKS AND OF PEOPLE'S
EXPERIENCES

From reading books and reflections of people on experiencing the death of loved ones, there is a consensus that
people manifest a variety of reactions when they are faced
with the loss of a dear one. These reactions can vary in the
order in which they manifest as different people grieve in
different ways and at different times.

In his book *Life After Death*, author Tony Cooke

approaches this important topic from the perspective of a pastor and a counsellor. He discusses biblical perspectives of grief as well as his practical involvement with grieving people. Cooke affirms that God permits his children to mourn but instructs them to mourn in a distinct way, a way that shows that they know God. For example, he advises that we can thank God in the situation since all our earthly relationships will end. We will all leave this earth at some point, but we can thank God that we will meet again in heaven.

Grieving is completely biblical and there are instances where even the apostles encouraged believers to mourn with one another:

> *Rejoice with those who rejoice; mourn with those*
> *who mourn. Romans 12:15*

He also cited the instance of Jesus weeping at the death of Lazarus even though he knew he would raise Lazarus from the dead (John 11:35). This instance underscores the importance of identifying emotionally with grieving people rather than attempting to deny or diminish these feelings. It also shows that outward display of emotions is not a lack of faith.

Cooke goes on to share practical experiences from bereaved church members as well as other people he has counselled in their grieving process. He describes the way people react as 'stunned', 'disbelief' and 'life seems unreal'.

He went further to discuss grieving as a process by citing Granger Westberg's Good Grief's ten stages of recovery from the loss of a loved one[2]:

1. Shock
2. Expression of emotion
3. Depression and loneliness
4. Physical symptoms of distress

5. Panic
6. Guilt
7. Anger and resentment
8. Reluctance to return to normal
9. Hope returns
10. Affirming a new reality

Other authors are quick to point out that this range of reactions is not fixed and the order in which a person manifests them also varies.

Another author and pastor, Wes Richards shares the story of grieving from his, and his family and church's experience of his wife's suffering and death in his book, *Hope and a Future*. In this poignantly told story, Richards charts the path to hope and restoration during and after the death of his beloved wife, Carol. There seem to be certain elements in the reaction stages that are related to those in the others summarised above.

Although they had all held hands and prayed together immediately after she breathed her last showing that their faith was anchored on the assurance that Carol was at home and at peace with God, faith and submission to God did not prevent natural grieving reactions.

Richards describes his and his children's reaction a few moments after the death of his wife in words that are similar to some of the stages of grief already discussed:

Mel was the first to leave the room. I went after her and found her sitting alone on a chair in the middle of the garden. She was holding her head in her hands. She looked utterly bereft. She wanted to be left alone. I went back upstairs to find Wes in *tears*. I held him tight and cried with him. James looked in a *daze*. I hugged him close too[3] (Emphasis mine)

He went on to describe his own reaction

I don't know how long I was there, but I *cried* and *sighed* a lot. I looked at her thin and ravaged body and felt a sense of *relief* that my lovely wife was no longer in pain. But oh God! How empty it already seemed without her. [4] (Emphasis mine)

Richards went on to describe the process of recovery with a focus on the blessings that God brought into their family after the death of his wife.

This amazing story of love, suffering and death is laced with the celebration of their three children's marriages to three siblings across continents. Richards' focus on thankfulness to God for Carol's life, the closeness with his children, and the blessings of their marriage and ministry helped his family's grieving and healing process.

In *Instantly a Widow* author Ruth Sissom describes her personal journey through grief after she lost her husband. She speaks of her immediate reaction at being told that her husband had died:

It seemed he yelled those words that felt like a huge sword cutting me from head to toe. The feeling of a powerful weight crushing down on me took my breath away" [5]

She says her first response was numbness especially as she had kissed him goodbye only a few hours before his accidental death. She writes that she also felt the peace of God flood her as soon as she called on God to help her:

"This must be the "peace that passes understanding" God promises to His children. It was completely beyond my

comprehension how I could experience absolute perfect peace in the midst of this chaos and emotional upheaval. I want to stay here forever basking in the warmth of God's peace and love,..."*Thank you, God, for this wonderful assurance that I am Your child and You love me.*" It is really true that "the Lord is near to the broken hearted and saves those who are crushed in spirit."[6] All emphasis in the original text.

However, she says the peace and calm assurance was not continuous and she went through some of the stages of grief outlined by Granger Westberg. Ruth describes the numbness at the morgue, the anger at both Cecil and the accident that took him, and the anger at friends and church members who said the wrong words, attempting to comfort her. She recounts questioning God's goodness, the distancing from friend and colleagues, and the loneliness especially at night-time. She also mentions feeling guilty about many issues ranging from selfishness at not wanting to care for a paralysed spouse; quarrels not settled; vacations she put off; and times she spent at work instead of with Cecil. Acknowledging her dependence on God and the support of family, friends, and church members, she reflects that she fluctuated between different emotions especially in the early days:

> I wanted to be strong – to rise above the pain, fears, panic, and confusion and show others I have a faith that doesn't crumble no matter what happens. I wanted to smile and sing with confidence It is Well With My Soul, but instead I'm afraid, weak, and utterly distraught. I feel You [God] have forsaken me. I feel like a terrible failure 'The joy of the Lord is your strength' is meaningless to me now. I'm trying so hard to put on a good front and not let people know how

I'm hurting inside. Then some word or song or picture triggers the grief and the sorrow flows over me like an ocean wave, and I'm lost in despair. Where are you, God? I've come to the bottom. If You give me one more thing, however tiny, I CAN'T TAKE IT![7] (emphasis in the original)

Derek Prince in his book, *Hope Beyond Grief* sensitises the believer to the grim reality and inevitability of death. Combining his experience as a pastor and a two-time widower, he challenges believers to put death and grief in their proper perspectives. He criticises present day culture's denial and softening of death on the one hand whilst he encourages the believer to treat death as a defeated enemy that it is. From the point of view of scripture, Jesus' death and resurrection is a big blow to death's claim to finality of a believer's life, he writes. Having the knowledge that death is more a rite of passage to a new life than a final closure of life should encourage believers to prepare for their own death and be comforted when they lose a loved one. Believers should face death with the confidence that Jesus who has redeemed them is resurrected and has promised both they and their loved ones who die in Christ the same resurrection. This is similar to the views expressed by one of the speakers at Ravi Zacharias's memorial service when he said Ravi's bed felt like 'a launching pad'[8] not a death bed.

Prince went on to discuss his experience after the death of his two wives. Even though he experienced immense pain, he writes that his trust and knowledge of God's purposes for the life of a believer helped him to stay strong. He also mentions that his losses made him better positioned to help people who were going through the grieving period as he was able to offer counsel based on his personal experience. His counsel to grieving people included:

1. Trust God's love and wisdom
2. Yield your loved one to God
3. Reaffirm your faith
4. Express your emotions
5. Lean on your fellow believers
6. Continue to serve Christ as faithfully as you can[9]

Prince concludes the book with his expectation of death and entering the presence of God rather than a dread of death. He also encourages believers to anticipate death with an assurance free of doubt and fear.

Sharing her experience at her husband's deathbed, Susan Lenzkes says that every 'thorn' experience in the life of a believer is a prelude to victory and relates her immediate reaction to the loss of her husband as part of the fruit of this belief:

> I will probably never experience a moment in life when I feel deeper pain or keener joy than I did in that terrible, wonderful moment. I saw him leave his body along with his last gasping breath, felt the cold, frightening finality of death... like someone slamming the door on laughter and love. Sobs burst from within me at the horror of sin's ultimate stabbing. Then joy erupted from the well of my soul, bathing my sorrow in waves of gratitude. As I wept, I sobbed, "Thank You! Thank You! Oh thank You, dear Jesus, for Your cross! Thank You for the empty tomb." This implausible, outrageous joy let me see and know in the deepest most hurting part of my soul that Herb had passed from this life to life everlasting. This was not the end! Everything in me was awash in the pain and wonder of that truth.[10]

My friend Alison also shared the experience of seeing her mother immediately after she died:

So, my first reaction to seeing that Mum had died was a sense of awe and wonder, like we were treading on holy ground.

Though Alison had spent the last two precious weeks with her mother and had the opportunity to say farewell and sing hymns to her, she describes her experience of grief:

Grief for me included extreme tiredness, not wanting to return to 'normal' life, the need to sleep lots and inability to plan and organise our family. And tears at the beginning and when remembering her. And craving green places, hills, trees, rivers, peaceful countryside places. Inability to cope with social occasions.

On the last point, Alison did miss my graduation because she could not cope with social occasions. But I made sure I went to her house to get a picture with her before I returned the graduation robe.

The renowned evangelist, Smith Wigglesworth[11] reporting on his response to the death of his wife wrote that his wife had told him that she got so near to heaven when preaching that she would be gone to heaven one day. After she finished preaching one night, she was found dead at the door. Wigglesworth knew that his wife had got what she wanted. Nevertheless, this preacher whose ministry had been known to include raising the dead commanded death to give his wife up. Continuing his account, he said the wife came back to life briefly, but God told him that she had finished her work on earth. Wigglesworth understood what God meant so he did not argue with God but let go. He confirmed with his children that they knew that the body that lay before them no longer housed their mother. At that point, he said that if we believe what Paul says, that going away is better than remaining in the body, we won't go about mourning loved ones when they die. He advises that we release our loved ones to God when he wants to take them.

When the death of loved ones happens, people grieve in different ways though some patterns have been identified. Some Christians, e.g. Wigglesworth and Finney (in Chapter 3) have reported totally different reactions. But generally, grieving is expected when a loved one dies, but believers in Christ are advised to grieve as though they know that there is a reunion in heaven.

If it was possible to choose
Then I'll make a choice
But choice is always possible
If I allow myself to choose
No one can stop me but I
I choose to make my choice now
To be prepared for what may
To not be wreaked by surprise
- *Olubusola Eshiet*

Forewarned is forearmed[1].

3: CHOICES

'I'll miss you'. That little sentence, some of us have had to say it many more times than others when a loved one is leaving us on journeys short or long.

I have a large and very international family. Two of my children, and one of my brothers live in Canada – three different provinces. My husband and I live in the United Kingdom. So, you can imagine how many times we have needed to say that little sentence. As if that were not enough, the rest of my siblings and my husband's live in different cities in Nigeria and so I would require a long-term visit to be able to have meaningful times with each of them and their families whenever I go to Nigeria. We have a strong extended family system also, so I have numerous aunties, uncles, cousins, nephews and nieces.

My cherished friends live in many different countries and sometimes we pay visits to one another. So, we meet to part and part to meet again.

Although these are my circumstances, goodbyes are hard for me. This is not my preferred lifestyle.

Let me focus on one of those several occasions of 'I'll miss you'.

In March 2000, my husband went on a work trip to the US. He was going to be gone for six weeks, our first long parting. I would be okay, I kept assuring myself. But I was so disappointed that I was not. I wept most of the time. I tried to remind myself again and again that he would be back, he was not dead, he had a return ticket, etc. Nothing worked. I lived like a widow for the six weeks.

You may need a reminder that those were not days of mobile phones and landlines were not commonplace where I lived. Emails were just making their debut and you had to handwrite your messages, like a letter to put in the post, and you went to a cybercafe where you would join a fairly long queue for a turn to send an email. When it was finally your turn, maybe after two hours of waiting, you gave your message to the cybercafe personnel who then typed in full view of others on the queue. Considering how much privacy attended the messages, how much could one write into such emails? When they were done typing your message on the computer, they clicked on the send button. If you were fortunate, it was sent, and it went to the recipient. Sometimes, it returned undelivered to the recipient for some strange reason! Maybe the network connection broke or simply the café personnel had written the recipient's address incorrectly. Sometimes you would not be told that the mail was not delivered so you would not ask for a refund or take too much time on the queue and slow down their business. However, if you were that fortunate that the email went through, you then went home and waited a day or two to go back to the café, where maybe there was a reply for you. You waited your turn again and as usual, the café staff helped you sign into your email account and they checked if you had a reply. If you did, hurray! They would call it up and print for you. Of course, calling up your message meant it stayed on the screen for all to read while the café staff worked their way around getting the email printed – another procedure.

I could write a book about all the attempts we made then to reach each other via phone and emails. Of course, my husband returned, and life went on. At the end of that experience, I told myself 'never again, Busola' and 'you must find a way to hold yourself together, to cope'.

As I said, that was only the first long parting. We have had many more partings since then including three years when I lived in the United Kingdom and my husband lived in Nigeria. During those three years, we visited often but we had periods as long as three months when there were no visits. I miss my husband anytime he is away, or when I go away (I have done more of the going away in recent times). I don't look forward to our being apart and would do as much as I can to prevent such. I miss my friends deeply when we visit and leave; miss my children and grandchildren, nieces and nephews, siblings, parents, etc. I usually describe myself as a people person. Being with my folks means a lot to me and parting from them can still sometimes be a very emotional matter. They don't all know this, but if they read this book they will now find out.

OTHERS SHARE THEIR PAIN OF PARTING

Writing this book has given me the sweet privilege of knowing other people who feel pained at parting from loved ones no matter how temporary the parting is, so it does appear I am not alone. Below are some ways people describe the pain of temporary parting:

> I have experienced missing someone as a physical pain, like a stomach ache. Every time my dearest

friend used to visit for a weekend and then leave after the visit for a day, I would experience a pain in my stomach. We used to bond in a very intellectual way, and I used to miss the way we talked together because it was a very particular way that we used to talk together.

I miss someone by feeling a sense of loss at the times we spent together and the things we did together. It could be as specific as missing the voice, the space the person occupies whether in the home or in my mind, the feeling that there is an aspect of me that is incomplete without that particular person.

I miss my husband in different ways. For example, I have been used to sleeping beside him and I miss him in that space. I miss his quiet assurance which makes me feel a sense of calm. I miss his voice and the way he will ask me if I want him to make me a cup of tea and which flavour I wanted (I love tea – different flavours). I miss the holding hands together to pray and the discussions about bible passages we read together and his sermons. We still do some of that when we are apart but you can't avoid feeling like we are talking across a divide.

I feel some headaches, slight fever, smarting eyes resulting from sleeping late because we need to catch up on things daily. Sometimes I feel listless especially if I am not able to reach him and I will keep wondering what is going on with him and if he was okay....

A SENSE OF CHOICE?

It often happens that when we take our annual holiday, we visit many family members and friends in the countries I have mentioned and more. So, on one trip, we may meet more than a hundred loved ones in their different locations so, more than one hundred goodbyes. This situation will continue for many more years if not all my lifetime. I don't want to continue to feel such deep pain at parting. So, I told myself, I needed to develop some coping strategies. I had to work out something. I decided to give myself a choice even though I didn't know how that would work out. I had boldly declared 'never again' but how to work that out was another process.

I chose to give myself some level of control on how I allow myself to experience the pain of parting. That seemed odd to me, to control the pain of the absence of someone I love. Would I just be pretending not to miss them so deeply? If it is not pretence, would choosing not to miss them with as much pain reduce the depth of my love for them? I somehow resolved the two issues by answering 'no' to the two questions. I told myself that it is a matter of the will, and I set to work on my plan.

When I faced parting from my husband, I would start thinking of things of interest that would keep me busy, engage my time effectively, and utilise my emotions – I have always had much of those. I also planned to spend any available time with people in my life who are accessible at such a time and by now you know I am blessed with many such people everywhere I find myself. Engaging with people has become even better now that mobile phones, emails and other means of communication are readily accessible. But even before the availability of those means of communication, I had made good my decision to be in control of the dreadful situation of parting.

When parting from friends and family, I would tell myself in advance that this is a short parting, no matter how long we part for, we will meet again.

I soon discovered that when I took control of the situation, I was able to decide how I would allow myself to feel the absence of my loved ones. I am constantly making decisions – I can choose joy at the opportunity to spend time with friends and family over complaining that we are parting, I can encourage myself and them with the hope of seeing again soon or sometime in the future instead of feeling bad that they are leaving. Now, I rejoice over the rare privilege of reuniting physically even for a few minutes rather than whine that the time is too short. I give and receive hugs (pre COVID-19 and hopefully soon again) quickly and generously, as the one main thing we cannot share by phone. I would even tell my mother that I can visit with her for only two hours knowing that such a short period is sufficient to give and receive all the hugs I will need in the next couple of months, even years, when we can share other aspects of our lives by phone.

Now, I seem to have a switch or, more accurately, a tap regulator through which I determine the amount of emotion to expend on each parting experience. I wish this were so all the time. However, I do have some level of control. In exercising this control, I am convinced that I am not unfeeling; there is no loss of love or intensity of care, only a care of myself in addition to the love for them. I will share a recent experience of parting as a confirmation of the control I sometimes have over these temporary partings.

Recently, my friend and her daughter temporarily relocated, spending four months with us in our city. It was reminiscent of our younger years when we lived in the same part of a city and saw each other every day. Conscious of my blues at parting, I began to prepare myself for their departure before they had even arrived. I told myself that we would use every moment available so that we wouldn't have to wish we had spent the time in a better way. We did all the things we used to do together then – took daily walks, cooked, talked about events as they happened, prayed, listened to bible teachings, went to the same church and she joined the same small group[1] in church as me. It was unbelievable that we could have such a time again, a precious gift, and we did not let any moment slip by. We intentionally made use of every possible moment to do things together. As the time approached for them to leave, I told myself and my friend that I would not whine at their departure but I had chosen to be thankful for the great and incredible opportunity we had to re-experience our earlier days. And so, we dropped them off at the airport and said our goodbyes, I left dry eyed, and returned home to my daily schedule like any other day. My cousin who knew what impact the parting could have on me phoned me to check that I was okay, and I told him I was fine. So, we can control our feelings and we are always making choices about them if we allow ourselves to do so.

Again, I found some feel good factor while interviewing people for this book. I feel I'm in good company with responses as below:

> Yes the feelings of missing my husband are controllable especially if I try to calm myself down and talk to myself to accept the reality that we cannot be together now. We both agreed on set times to pray. If we started the day with praying and catching up on what each person would be doing, then the anxiety of wondering what he was doing was reduced. Moreover, when I get busy with what I needed to do, I do not

keep my mind on him all through that time. I go on knowing that we have a set time to catch up again later in the day.

We agreed on issues we can discuss while apart and things that can wait until we are together again. We both agreed not to argue about things and to maintain good nutritional habits and mental health.

Another response:

I think being busy and active has been my normal way of dealing with temporary pain and in the case of my friend, the business of living daily life meant that the pain would just fade away.

I found similarities in these responses to my decision on how I would miss people. I find shared ideas like: 'calm myself down' 'pray together', 'accept the reality that we cannot be together now', 'being busy', 'maintain good nutritional habits and mental health' and 'we agreed'.

Several people agree that it is possible to control the pain of missing our loved ones when they are temporarily absent. It is obvious that the control factor involves a choice, a decision. It does not happen by chance or wishful thinking. This leads to the next big thought on my mind: if this ability to make a choice may in any way be applicable to missing a loved one who dies and so, how we mourn our loss. .....

Were/are these feelings and pains (of grief) controllable or manageable? Remarkably, everyone interviewed agreed that the pains of grief are controllable. The one person, Jummy, who thought she could not control herself found out that she could. Her words:

At the beginning, they were not (controllable). I could not stop crying all day and night. I kept thinking about my mum and imagining her in the different parts of the apartment where she used to sit and how she used to play with the children. As time went on however *(within days)* and then I got sick, I began to think of the ways I can manage my emotions and feelings. (Emphasis mine)

Here are some of the responses I got from people to the questions: What did/do you try to do to manage or control the pain? Has/did any of these worked in helping you control the pain?

I forced myself to do what I needed to do e.g. taking care of the children and moving my mind from the pain. I started attending a fellowship of others who were widows where people shared their experiences and how they were able to cope with their griefs. Praying and telling God exactly how I was feeling. Sharing with friends and close ones how I was feeling. Being involved and busy with ministry work helped to remove my mind. Reading the word of God and dwelling on God's promises and love for me.

Went for a walk in Ingram Valley! Talked with friends who had been through the same thing. Talked about Mum – didn't avoid talking about her. And then I wrote about her and that helped enormously. It was probably what helped the most. And I wrote poetry about that period of time while she was dying.

I began to think of all the good times I had with my mum, all the things she used to say and how much her words and attitude formed me. I began to think that she accepted that she might not survive the sickness long before any of us did. She encouraged us and I felt that she was brave, why shouldn't I? I kept repeating to myself that "memories are made of those." I even began to smile when I remembered some of the things she would say. I did not even know when I began to say "my mum would always say or do----." I never really used those when she was alive. Also, I started accepting that she has transited to someone I will always remember fondly, someone whose calmness and contentment wins at the end. My feistiness is a character trait I inherited from my dad but I needed to be reminding myself that I am Edith's daughter so nothing should ever go overboard. This way, I am able to reduce the pain of missing her. Finally, I am happy that I look like her so actually a lot more people remember her when they see me, including my siblings.

I began to feel thankful that I was able to go and "say" goodbye to my dad with my husband and daughter. I was also thankful that he saw one of his children "live abroad", in fulfilment of his wish even though I regretted that he was too old to visit me. I was also thankful that he died the way he did – without needing someone to care for his personal hygiene and similar needs because he was one man that would not have wanted to be treated as an invalid in sickness. I was relieved that we had an opportunity to deliberately present the gospel of salvation again to him and led him in a prayer of salvation three weeks before he died. I felt that he was happy and that his children were around him when he died. I felt a sense of closure.

Focus on the word of God about the dead and the living. Coming to reality that we all are just strangers in this planet Earth. Believing that, those who died in Christ Jesus, have left the imprisonment of this world to the enjoyment of the world beyond. I have to remember that there are many people looking up to me, so if don't control myself, I will discourage many or facilitate others to continue to wallow in misery. I also have to submit to divine sovereignty.

I started going out to meet people. I also started coming to church and participating in the activities I used to enjoy at church. I sing at church but after my mum's death, I was so depressed and disillusioned that I started isolating myself from people and from any social activity. But now I feel relaxed when I am with other people. I also feel some comfort from singing and hearing other people sing too. The sermons and readings from the bible are all comforting. Moreover, I feel that people are praying for me and that they do care for me. Everyone is encouraging me to socialise more and people invite us to their homes for meals after church. All these have been immensely helpful.

Charles Finney wrote about the death of his wife in his auto-biography. After a dialogue between Finney and God where God asked Finney if he loved his wife for her sake or just for himself; and if he loved her for the Lord's sake or just for his (Finney's) sake, God then asked him why Finney would think only on his loss instead of her gain and why he would not rejoice with the fact that she was with God, happy and joyful. Finney said the feeling that came over him was indescribable and he had an immediate change in his state of mind and from then on, he no longer had any sense of sorrow. All this was because he knew that his wife wasn't dead but alive and enjoying the beauty of heaven.[2]

It would appear from the responses above and many others that even during periods of deep sorrow, mourners are making choices. A more informed person may be able to make those choices earlier and this may be helpful to the mourner. For example, Jummy above, said she was crying day and night until she took ill:

> As time went on however *(within days)* and then I got sick, I began to think of the ways I can manage my emotions and feelings.

Jummy may have been spared some crying and hospitalisation if she had known that she could control her feelings of loss. Ijeoma validates this when she said:

> If we understand that we can control our emotions and that God has made provision for healing, I might have healed faster but no one tells you that directly.

Finney, mentioned above, used words like 'feelings' and 'state of mind'.

Both Jummy and Finney described a change in their thinking and in the way they felt. Even though the changes were driven by different reasonings, each change involved a decision to do things differently as a result of a shift in attitude.

Below are some of the ways people sought to control their grief:

- Doing things they like to do: took a walk, sing in the choir, fellowship, writing poetry, stories.
- Being busy
- Participating in church and support group activities
- Spending time with friends and family and sharing their feelings with them.
- Talking about the deceased
- Thinking of good times shared with the deceased
- Focusing on the Bible for comfort especially remembering that the dead in Christ is in a better place.
- Sense of fulfilling responsibility to others - children, church members, staff,
- Submitting to God's sovereignty
- Knowledge that they are being prayed for.

Can these experiences be turned into choices when grief comes? Is it possible to think in advance on how to use the ways people got relief for getting relief for ourselves when such times come to us? What would I do if the unexpected happens to my parents, friends, child, spouse? In my experience, these are not pleasant questions to ask oneself, but it can be helpful to ask so that one is not massively shocked at something that should be expected though it is usually most unexpected.

Admire soon enough
Celebrate soon enough
Care soon enough
Praise soon enough
Soon it'll be too late
And it won't be soon enough
To admire, celebrate, care and praise
- *Olubusola Eshiet*

*There is an appointed time for everything. And there is a time for
every event under heaven — a time to give birth, and a time to die.
Ecclesiastes 3:1-2 (NASB)*

4: PREPARING TO LET GO

Since grief is a sure event in our lives, and there are sufficient examples of those who have gone the way of grief before us, and maybe even our own personal examples, are we able to learn from these examples or does experience have to always retain the prestigious place of being the best teacher?

In this chapter, I will look at some practical steps we can take to demystify grief and to prepare for it.

The statistics of death is that "one out of every one still dies"[1].

It doesn't happen in a chronological manner, so anyone can die before the other.

The expected end of pregnancy is the birth of a baby or babies (although sadly, there are sometimes a few exceptions to the fulfilment of this expectation). The truth of the matter is that the expected end of that baby that is born through the pregnancy is death, no exception.

We prepare for birth - paint a room, buy clothes, get ready to visit, we do baby showers, we talk about the progress of baby's growth in the womb to friends and family, we share pictures of scans on our social media, sometimes we move houses to bigger or more comfortable ones, and we even buy more roomy cars. We attend pre-natal classes, speak to people who have had babies before, and search online resources to learn as much as we can to prepare ourselves for the baby. We try to learn all we can about how to live joyfully with the baby. The baby should be comfortable around us and we desire to be comfortable around them. Although the expectation of the new member of the family brings joy, we agree that our lives will never be the same as before the baby came. So, we anticipate the changes that the arrival will bring into our lives and we prepare our minds for the additional expenses and tasks (sleepless nights) that will be occasioned by the birth. We chat to other members of the family (even our little children) about the expected little one. We invite our toddler to touch and speak to the baby (baby bump) so even the youngest member of the family is in a state of expectation of the new little brother or sister.

Such and more are the extent to which we prepare for the arrival of a baby, justifiably so, as a new member is coming into the family and into the world. We think about the pregnancy, we talk about it and we take action.

My challenge is for people to begin to do these three things about death:

Think, Talk, Take Steps.

THINK

Do we think even for a moment about the possibility of losing people we love to death even though death is as sure as and even surer than birth? Why has the most expected event become the unexpected? Why do we go about life as if we will remain here forever with all our family members, friends, colleagues, etc? Could it be because death seems 'abnormal'? Indeed, the creation account reveals that death is 'abnormal'. Death was not a part of the creation plan. Death came because humans disobeyed God.

> *The Lord God took the man and put him in the Garden of Eden to work it and take care of it. And the Lord God commanded the man, "You are free to eat from any tree in the garden; but you must not eat from the tree of the knowledge of good and evil, for when you eat from it you will certainly die." Genesis 2:15-17*

Also Ecclesiastes 3:11 says that God has set eternity in the heart. Little wonder we have the desire to live together forever. However, since death has become a part of life as we know it, it is important to think about death.

If we turn the above scenario of expecting the birth of a baby around a bit, just from thinking of birth (beginning of life) to thinking of death (end of life), we would be thinking this way if we allow ourselves to do so:

If my spouse, friend, sibling, child (I shuddered even more as I wrote the last one) dies before I do, it will be an incredibly sad event. I will quickly inform friends and family; I will put the information on my social media so that it travels fast. I will share our favourite pictures with my friends, family, and followers. In the case of my husband, I think I will move to a smaller house because this house will become too big for me. In fact. I may prefer an apartment building because I will more likely see people in the hallways and at the entrance so have more opportunities for quick chats than if I live in a house alone.

I love my daily walks so will go for walks in our favourite parks; it is likely that fresh air and recollections of all the nice times we had in those parks will bring some moments of joy. Life will never be the same again and I will always miss them but I will still be here and so I need to be comfortable and in good health. I will call my friends (put some names in) anytime I feel too low to continue. Thankfully, they are in different time zones so someone will be awake almost anytime I need a friend. And I am blessed with many friends and family members. I am blessed, yes, to have met so many good people in my life and I keep investing in those relationships and new ones. I am deliberate about making friends across all age brackets. I can call one of many people and I can be sure to get one or two who will be available to speak to me any time I am distressed and lonely. If I cannot sleep, I will speak to one of them till I sleep off on them. They will be happy to support me so they will not mind that I left them on the phone.

When I lack the interest in eating or even in cooking, I will call a friend or family member on video and chat to them as I cook. If I need to engage more than one person, I will make a group call of two such persons who can cook with me and can even eat when I am eating.

I can and will invite a friend along on a walk, physically or by phone. I do so now, why not then.

The best of all is that I can talk to God anytime. I hear from people who have grieved that I may not even feel like speaking to God at some point. I hope this does not happen to me, but I am not afraid if it does because God will not turn me back. At any time, I am able to speak to him. He will not scold me for not feeling like praying earlier but will always welcome me with open arms. I do not need to book an appointment in advance. I am welcome anytime of the day or night, so I will pray anytime I can. And I can call a friend to pray with me. If I cannot pray, I know friends will be praying for me.

Also, I will play worship music and sing along, I love songs and singing, and dancing. So, I will dance when I can. And I will listen to my favourite Bible teachers online – I have many of them.

What about being happy for my dead loved one as they are now in a better place? I hope I can be as selfless as to rejoice with them. I do not feel that way for now, but I guess I can work on myself as part of preparation.

Wait a minute, are there physical or online courses that prepare people for loss of loved ones? I should enrol in one of those and learn as much as possible about loss and grief. I think I will speak with my colleague whose brother died a few years ago about what that involved for him; hopefully, he will be willing to talk about it. Yes, we should hang out for coffee so I ask him what to do if such should ever happen to me. Oh, this is going to be so extremely sad if it ever happens, but it just may, so I need to prepare.

How did you feel reading the above? Do you think you can bring yourself to begin to think this way? Death has been treated as a taboo and so something to avoid thinking about. In some cultures, including my growing up Christian culture, it is even said that such thoughts may bring about the death of a loved one. I challenge the culture that holds you back from taking constructive steps about the things that come to your mind and that you know are the realities of life. The thoughts certainly do not cause the death of the loved one. If they did, my husband would no longer be alive. But he is!

Talking with some close friends has brought me to the conclusion that the fear of loss I described earlier is not limited to only me, it may be a bit more widespread than I imagined but most people keep the thoughts to themselves as I did.

My friend, Bunmi told me that she had always thought about the possibility of her husband dying before she does although she wishes it is otherwise. (She is not alone in so wishing.) She wonders what would become of the family's business which her husband has grown into a prosperous one. Will they lose the company to the staff as no member of the family works with him in the company? She is in a blossoming profession which she would not leave to learn how he runs the business. So, if he dies sooner than they wished, she and her children's sorrow will not be only about losing his companionship but will extend to losing the business that he spent many years building. This would be sad indeed. But she didn't leave it at that point. Though she would not leave her job to take up a role in her husband's business, and none of her children was likely to do so, she did the only thing she knew to do about it – she prayed. That, by the way, is the most powerful thing to do about every situation. God's answer may not always be predictable, but he always gives peace and offers direction. In my friend's case, he answered the prayers in a way she could not imagine. Though she didn't share her thoughts with her family, one of their children decided to take reduced hours on the job they currently do and join their father on his business. The child said to the mother, 'I don't know why I have been wasting my time searching for a job when I can work with my father. I spend my time building others' business when I can do that for our own business.' You can imagine my friend's joy at this. Because my friend expected answers to her prayer, she knew that her child's decision was not a coincidence but an answer to prayers. She allowed herself to think of the unwanted possibility of her husband dying before she does. This led her to praying and the praying brought an answer to her worries. If she didn't think, she wouldn't have prayed.

TALK

As I mentioned in an earlier chapter, in the early years of my marriage, I was plagued by thoughts of the possibility of my husband not returning from one of his many trips. Roads were dangerous, planes crashed, angry mobs killed innocent people, he has never been a sickly person, but he has had his fair share of ill health. So, the raging question was, what if he died? If you read the Prologue, you won't be surprised that I didn't share these thoughts with anyone. No one would want to hear such thoughts; I would have been advised to reject them and think about life and the promises of God for a long life. Also, as the thoughts were about the only person I would have felt safe to share them with, my husband, I imagined that it was irrational to put such a burden on him. Looking back now, I wish I had told him; he would have been able to help me. Thank God that the truth of His word set me free from the fears that harassed me. Since then, and that has been many years, my husband and I speak freely about the death of any of us, and I speak freely of death with a few friends who are able to bear the thought of discussing the death of any of us or of our loved ones. I remember when a friend of our youngest child died about fifteen years ago. We gathered as a sorrowing family and told one another a few truths, especially that any of us could die and leave the others so we should all live together as if this could happen any day. Thankfully, we are all still alive.

So, I would say: talk about your death and their death with loved ones, it will not kill either you or them! A widow comments:

> I think talking about death would help. It's not something I consciously talked about with my late spouse except in situations of loss of someone we knew, or a movie brought it up. You should talk about it in happy times and sad times like when you have attended a funeral. (A funeral sets the atmosphere to discuss death because people are usually sober and tend to be philosophical).

Recently, I called my Mum and asked her questions to clarify some opinions I have about my early years. I did so because she is the only one who can tell me with all the details I needed, not my Dad. She is the keeper of dates and days and I thought I may well ask her now that I still have her. I did an audio recording of the call so that I would not lose any detail to forgetfulness. When I played some of it back to her, she said 'you recorded my voice for when I'm gone?' That was not the reason why I recorded her voice, but she had just given me an idea. I would be able to play this to my grandchildren in future, and to myself as a reminder of my mum. The thought causes my stomach to tighten as I write. So, you see, this is not the writing of someone who has attained but someone who is on a journey. I will be getting more recordings of my mum's voice, I told her so.

My Grandma (Mama) was a woman who talked about her death as naturally and as often as she spoke about her trips to the market. Mama would tell us which of her outfits each of us ladies should be dressed in, beginning with my mother, me the first grandchild, all the way to each/any of my four sisters who was old enough at the time of the discussion. More names were added as the girls grew old enough to wear Mama's size – though I don't remember that any of us dressed in Mama's attire during her funeral and I'm not sure what attire she recommended for my brothers. She lived for more than thirty years from the time I started hearing her speak about her death. I would say that Mama laid a foundation of thinking and talking about death for me but not the fear that accompanied it for me at first. Mama spoke of her death with joy and she looked forward to meeting her Saviour. She died at 88.

Later, my Mum, happy that she had done the last service for her mother, began talking to us freely about her own death. My father also talked about his death especially every time a friend or age mate died. Both are still alive; Mum at 78 and Dad at 83. Surely, talking about death does not hasten the coming of death.

My friend, Bunmi, and I found it very natural talking about the possibility of death. For example, we recently had the following conversation: 'I told my husband he shouldn't think of dying before me. He has been carrying me and my burdens since I was in my late teens. If he leaves me, who will be my burden bearer?' And I said to her, 'aren't you selfish, he has been carrying you for this long and you still want him to carry your corpse?' We both laughed.

The discussion with Bunmi may appear strange to many, just as it would have to me years ago. As friends, shouldn't we have a good time talking about the present, and plan for the bright futures that lie ahead of us? Why discuss such grim matters?

I suggest that friends and family members, young and old add talks about the possible death of any of them to their regular talk times.

I found that people are most uncomfortable talking about death or don't think it is something to ever discuss. As Bill Crowder wrote:

.... in our culture and in our day, we do whatever we can to avoid the subject of death. And usually it is at funerals, memorial services, or celebrations of life (or whatever the current phrase of culture may be) that we are dragged, kicking and screaming, to a moment where we must come face-to-face with death.[2]

Ijeoma affirms the cultural aversion to talking about death and calls on the Church to talk more about death:

I agree that we need to demystify death but who will do that for us. In a way I see culture of our society overlapping with that of the church. The church ought to create awareness through teaching on the subject of death and not talk about it only at funerals.

For example, I discussed the idea of this book with another friend and she became distressed. I had to spend extra time with her to help her feel okay all the time I was thinking 'this can and will happen to you. You will lose friends and family members. I may even die before you and you would be here to grieve my leaving.' I hope I will have some other opportunity to help her come to terms with discussing the subject.

Recently, my husband and I were talking with our daughter on the phone and I shared something I just read on two memorial stones with her: 'When God gives a gift, he wraps it in a person.' She thought that was nice. The second one was: 'Mum, best friend'. I said to her that I desire that our relationship will remain such that she would write that about me. Her response, with laughter was: 'You won't tell me what to write about you.' When my husband and I tried to take the discussion a bit further, she promptly asked us why we are talking about death! Considering that she is a nurse and encounters the possibility of death regularly, one would have thought that she will freely discuss death in her family. We soon moved on to other topics of interest, but we were back to it again in another few days.

Talking about death is usually clothed in gloom. On the contrary, the discussions of final partings with my grandmother, parents, daughter, and friends mentioned above were not in depressing circumstances. They were usually lively, loving chats occasioning laughter and all other elements one can hope to find in an affectionate atmosphere.

Take Action (Do Something Now)

If I knew my friend was terminally ill, I would be praying for healing and expecting them to be healed. But I would prepare a visit to them if I possibly could. This doesn't negate faith in God. Our faith should be the kind that trusts God with all possible actions. A visit would warm both my friend's and my heart. And if God decides it is time for her to die, I would have given myself the wonderful privilege of saying goodbye to my friend and she would have the opportunity of receiving the assurance of my love and care again before she dies. If a visit isn't possible, we could chat on phone and be real to each other about the impending parting.

When I called my friend, Melrose (a widow) to share the idea of this book with her, I said to her: 'if you call my phone and it repeatedly fails to ring, you would call Emmanuel to ask where I am. Do you realise that it is possible he tells you I'm gone; I died some days ago?' As usual, Melrose's first reaction was 'God forbid' but she quickly came back to herself and said to me: 'I don't have Emmanuel's phone number, please send it to me in case I need it.'

So, we talked, and we acted. I sent her my husband's phone number.

Possible Actions

There are many practical things we could be doing to help us prepare for death of loved ones.

1. *Identify and consciously enjoy now the things you like about them*

This may mean taking thoughts of what you value/enjoy about them. Below are some answers people gave to the questions: 'What made them special to you?' and 'What things do you miss about your loved one?'

My husband showed to me, his caring attitude, his understanding and patience towards me, the feeling of being cared and loved by someone special, his physical presence and companionship, someone to share daily experiences with, someone to care for and love, the help he rendered to me in my areas of weaknesses (e.g. fixing things around in the house). He made me feel very special and understood me very well, showed me very practical love. He was a friend that I could easily share my feelings with. He was very tolerant and patient with my weaknesses. He was a good father to my children. He loved and served God dearly. He was a model of who a true Christian is.

She was my mother. It only dawned on me after she died how much she poured out her life into us. She showed sacrificial mother's love in a million different ways. I miss the gentle way she was involved with our children. I miss her being in the kitchen when we arrived at Mum and Dad's house. I miss her intuitive ability to feel our pains and sorrows, her generosity, resourcefulness, and creativity. Really, I just miss her as a whole person.

I miss my mother, the friendship that existed between us. I remember that I used to lie down on her bed with her and we would just talk. I missed the things she would say and how it would not be a big deal if I told her some bad things I had done. I missed her expectations of me.

I missed my dad as my cheer leader. I missed how my dad would make me feel there is nothing I cannot achieve in this life. I missed my dad's youthfulness and his way of adding flourish to whatever he wants to do and whatever he wants you to do for yourself or for him. Everything for him called for a big and loud celebration.

My daughter thought of others, she was caring, forward looking, easy going, hardly manifesting anger, non-belligerent, always smiling, never missed an opportunity to share a gift. She showed appreciation and gratitude. Manifested great willingness to obey instruction.

She was my mum. I miss my mum in every way possible. I miss her reassuring voice, her quiet way of moving about in the home and helping with everything. She was great with my children and they listened to grandma more than they listened to me.

She was always patient with them and yet firm where she needs to be. I miss her cooking different dishes in the kitchen. I miss her sacrificial lifestyle.

2. Pay attention to basic housekeeping.

One lady commented:

Yes, I was kind of stranded when my husband died because there were some things around the home that I could not do myself e.g. changing the gas cylinder when it finished, how to process bank transactions. It is good for spouses to make each other more capable of doing needful things in the house e.g. driving, taking care of things around in the house and cooking so that if any dies before the other, the person left behind will not feel stranded.

This doesn't mean that everyone must know how to do everything, but we could make ourselves more comfortable doing things that we can do and learning to do a few things that we don't already know how to do. The lady above did her bank transactions and managed a few technical matters like changing gas cylinders before she got married. I'm sure she was not alone in relinquishing some of those activities once she got married. Spouses often have a way of dividing up chores in the house such that one person has responsibility for a set of tasks and the other person for the other. If possible, each should know a bit of what the other person does. This would save one some unnecessary tears if the other suddenly dies. For example, this lady found herself in tears when confronted with carrying out some banking transactions soon after her husband died. If she knew her way around those transactions, she would have saved herself some tears. Her tears would have been for missing her husband's company but not when she needed to transfer funds from one account to the other or when she had to pay the children's school fees.

So, why not learn: how to cook that favourite dish; how the lawn mower works; how to change a bulb; how to make a budget etc.

Do you have the login details to important records? Suddenly feeling locked out of accounts that were managed by a spouse can be frustrating. Imagine needing to renew your home insurance and not knowing which company provides it. Taking care of these little details can provide extra peace of mind and reduce stress points in case of the death of a spouse.

3. *Spending time with loved ones.*

Make that visit. At times we plan to visit loved ones who live some distance away from us but we never seem to have the time, or in some cases the funds required for transportation to the friend or relative. Have you taken some thoughts about this? If this person were to die, will you have the time or funds needed to travel to their funeral? Is it not important to see them alive when we can have good times with them? Is it only when they die that it becomes essential to go and pay our last respects? I think 'living' respects are important too.

4. *Take that family trip*

How many times have you postponed that family trip? For years, you plan to make a trip as a family. You would explore the Grand Canyon, go to Singapore, ... But for some reason, you have never been able to carry it through. Next year will do, you always say.

Perhaps you planned to hold a family reunion with all

siblings and their children and the grandparents, but you always postpone it.

5. *Make/Take that phone call.*

Do you often reject calls from friends and family? And you never even call them back? Does it occur to you that you may wish to speak to them someday, but they will not be available because they are dead? You may wish you never rejected their calls and find yourself wishing to hear their voice. You may have deep regrets at the calls you rejected, and you may wish you called someone more frequently. Kim told me of deep regrets at not taking her uncle's call. She meant well and had hoped to call him back at the end of the month. However, before the month ended, she got a call from her brother informing her of her uncle's death. Allan was more fortunate; he responded to an urge to call his brother whom he had not spoken to in ages and they had a reunion call. In a few months, the brother died. Allan shared with me that he felt very happy that he made the call.

6. *Appreciate them*

Tell them what you appreciate about them. Often, we wait until someone had died before we tell the world how great they were. The poem that goes under different titles and authorship (*Love Me Before I Die*[3]; *Do it Now Instead*[4]) captures the heart of the matter. The dead cannot hear any of the good words we say about them, neither can they feel the smell of the flowers we take to their funeral. Telling them what you appreciate about them gives you the opportunity to make them happy. An additional benefit of telling them is that they will likely do more of what you appreciate, and you will have more things to value about them.

7. *Resolve issues quickly*

Unresolved issues can cause deep sorrow if a loved one dies and there would not be any opportunity to resolve them again.

8. *The paperwork is important too*

Get them to take up that life insurance, to write a will, to plan for funeral directors etc where applicable.

9. *Turn other people's regrets into action points*

"I wish I was more patient with him"

"I wish we sought another doctor's opinion"

Thinking creatively about regrets we have heard others express and taking positive actions about them may not prevent our loved ones from dying but would save us from regrets that we failed to do our best to keep them alive for longer. As Ijeoma said:

Experience doesn't have to be the best teacher if we avail ourselves of the experience of others.

People shared how helpful it was that they were prepared in some way for their relation's death:

I think we were prepared for Mum's death which helped enormously. It seemed to me that God's grace was readily available to us as a family and to me as an individual.

Vida in a talk about how she has coped with grief said:

Before they die, let us live life like the person is important to us right now. What I see people doing is that we go along our lives and the people important to us, we don't spend time with.

A lot of the times, people have issues because they haven't

resolved before the person died. They are mad at them; they are not at the right relationship with them, so my encouragement is that you make sure that you settle and resolve issues in your life. You know, make sure you are good with the people that are close to you so that if something happens, yes you are grieving; you don't like the fact that they are not with you again but you are at peace because you know they are with the Lord.

I think the key thing is that people don't resolve these things before that person that is important to them is dead. Why are you waiting until they are dead. You are the main one hurting...I wish I had done this, I wish I had done that. Take the time and make sure you get that resolved before they die.

Love them. Like my mum now, sometimes I just want to hug her real hard...I will have no regrets because I know that I am doing everything within my power to give her the quality life that she deserves... so when she goes on to be with the Lord, I am gonna miss her but I am gonna be okay. I have decided that in advance that I am gonna be okay[5]

Preparation could be compared to knowing that I may have physical pain or an injury at some point in life and so I keep a First Aid Kit in my home. I ensure I have some off-the-counter pain killer medication at home just in case I need it, or a guest needs it. Preparation of our minds can be compared to that First Aid Kit situation. We don't live in the fear of cutting ourselves with a knife just because we have plasters and band aids at home, neither do we live in the fear of having a headache because we have analgesics. In the same way, preparing our minds for times of loss and grief doesn't occasion the fear of loss; instead, it helps us live lives more confident that we are prepared for the expected. Also, keeping those first aid resources doesn't cause us to injure ourselves or fall sick. Likewise, preparing our minds for loss of dear ones doesn't cause the loss to happen.

Preparation makes it possible for us to live as if we are in the last moments with our loved ones and this helps us enjoy a more loving and peaceful life. This way, we'll be able to say when our loved one dies: 'with gratitude to God for a life spent with ....'

Hard partings, sad partings
Last partings, heart breaking
Undesirable, unstoppable
Sorrowful times
Departure times
- Olubusola Eshiet

The time of my departure has come. 2 Timothy 4

5: MY FELLOWSHIP WITH BEREAVEMENT

As I pondered writing this book, I had many discouraging thoughts. One of the thoughts was that I may not have had sufficient experiences of bereavement and so I may not be qualified to write a book on loss occasioned by death. Looking back now, I don't remember what level of experience I classified as sufficient. I have a line-up of bereavement experiences in my family and in my circle of friends.

However, I think the discouragement must have been because my personal experiences of bereavement may seem indirect to non-close family members unless I explain that I have a generational history of informal adoption of close family members. I have, with the support of my husband, been able to carry on this tradition. For example, I was 'adopted' by my grandmother as were two of my younger sisters, Sola and Aanu. She brought us up from our early years until each of us completed primary education. My stay with Mama overlapped briefly with Sola's stay but Aanu is ten years younger than me so I was long gone from home when she lived with Mama. Each of us may have continued living with Mama if there had been a good secondary school where she lived but as this was not so, we left her at about the completion of our primary education. By this arrangement, she had the main responsibility for our upbringing until we left her home and even when we left for secondary school, we always returned to her on holidays. Mama's home would almost always be my first point of call whenever I visited home (she was happy about this) and from her, I would proceed to my parents who lived about five kilometres away, in another town. Sola, Aanu and I are still referred to by our other siblings as 'Omo Mama', Mama's children, though all of us seven siblings are remarkably close and there is no mark of having been raised separately in our relationship with one another.

The type of relationship I have described about Mama also existed between my parents and a younger cousin of my dad's, Bode, who was just slightly older than me and who I write about in this chapter. So, it won't be a surprise that I had the kind of relationship with Ekemini that I relate later on in the chapter.

I have had my share of bereavement and grief and will relate some of them here. I will end the chapter with my reflections on these experiences.

Also, I have spent much time in close fellowship with people who mourn, mourning with them and feeling the deep sense of their grief with them. I have supported a few people in and maybe through the process of their grief. I referred to some of these experiences earlier when I talked about how hard I grieved when I had mourned with others. Some of them are still deep in mourning as I write, while others are at different stages of their grief and some have come through. It has been a privilege walking alongside people either briefly or for the long haul.

It is better to go to a house of mourning than to go to a

house of feasting, for death is the destiny of
everyone; the living should take this to heart.
Ecclesiastes 7:2

MY PERSONAL EXPERIENCE OF BEREAVEMENT AND GRIEF

Mama

I have mentioned my grandmother who was the first mother I knew. The lovely story of how I was blessed with two mothers would make up another book. Mama was always my mother, for and about whom I recited Ann Taylor's poem 'My Mother'[1]. When she started growing older (though to me, she was always old), I began to be conscious that she would die. Every visit was treated as a farewell visit where both of us clung to each other and looked at each other with that knowing look of 'this may be the last'. Mama would say if we didn't meet here again, we would meet at Jesus' feet. But the next time I would go to visit her, and we would rejoice at seeing each other again. She was always very joyful to see me and she spared no praises to God for allowing us to see each other again. That continued for years until one day, I returned from a trip - my sister, Funke, came over to my house and gave me a hug that felt different. As I was still trying to understand what was different about the hug, she told me that Mama was gone. I don't remember if I cried immediately but I did at the funeral and internment services and I have carried the hole of her absence in my heart since then. I can still see Mama standing just outside her house, waving goodbye.

Christine

Simon, a Christian brother, was my colleague at University and my husband's colleague at work. Those relationships set the stage for a deep friendship. Simon then introduced me to Christine, his wife. Christine and I developed a friendship and so our families were friends. We played, ate, and prayed together. We developed many common interests. Christine was pregnant with her fourth child and was near delivery. We talked and made plans for the arrival of the baby, exciting times. So, when Simon turned up at my door and told me 'your friend is dead, she died in childbirth', I was in a momentary daze but the practical side of me soon took over, especially having read 'Early Widow'. I arranged for him to inform his office, checked on the well-being of the children and did all I could to support my friend's husband, who also was my friend. I grieved for Christine for years and I kept close to the family. The children are adults now and our relationship with them and their father has continued to be close. It has since included their step-mum and step-siblings.

Ekemini, my son. He was my husband's nephew who became informally adopted into our nuclear family. He was close to us throughout his growing up years and after graduation from university, he made his home permanently with us. He was an intelligent, vibrant, God-loving, family-loving and resourceful young man. He struggled with asthma, but he didn't allow that deter him from reaching for the best. He was the best in everything he attempted, and the future lay before him. When I moved to the UK, we stayed in regular touch and he didn't fail to send me regular updates. Writing this portion caused me to look up our emails of December 2011. He came to the UK on a work trip, but we were away on vacation. We would have planned our trip differently, but we knew about his too late to make any changes to our plan. Who goes on an international training at Christmas, we would have thought? So, we planned to meet in February when I was booked to go to Nigeria. However, we exchanged several emails a day and called each other on phone, he was getting updates on our holiday and I was getting updates on his training and visits.

I was about to make that trip to Nigeria in February 2012; my bags were packed and waiting by the door as my taxi would come early the next morning. Just before I got into bed for what I hoped would be a restful night, I had a call from Austine, my kid brother; Ekemini was suffering from a bad attack of asthma and had been taken to the hospital. The next set of events happened as if in a jiffy. I hung on to the phone for hours, 'following' Austine from the first hospital to the second and in two hours, Ekemini was pronounced dead. I even 'followed' Austine to the morgue all the while hoping that God would do a miracle and that the doctors would have a change of verdict. There was no miracle of raising the dead this time, the body was deposited. Body? I couldn't even think of that or understand what that meant.

Dazed and confused were the words to describe my feeling. I even contemplated cancelling my trip but my husband encouraged me to make the trip. Not that cancelling it would have been any help but the question in my head was 'what is the point of travelling now, when I would not see Ekemini?' I think that trip was some mercy for me as it enabled me to participate in the funeral ceremonies of my dear son. I don't know how I got the strength, but I gave a farewell speech at his funeral service. I don't remember what I said but I was happy that I did that service for Ekemini. I cried for months. I would wake up in the night, sit on my bed and weep. I saw his face on so many people, especially young men around his age who dressed up in suits as he always did to work. Flight crew resembled him, bankers too, etc. Ekemini is unforgettable.

Bode (the most recent)

Bode was my brother. Our real relationship was that of cousins but only I, being the oldest, remember when he came to live with my parents; none of my siblings do. My parents 'adopted' him. He was always a part of the household. The only difference was that he had a different surname and was free to not go to church. His father was a Muslim. The rest of us had to go to church. Later in life, he changed his name to our family name, and he converted to Christianity. Bode's position in our family was oldest boy and I, oldest girl. When he got married, he and his family made their home with Mum and Dad for many years until he built his own house. Even then, he maintained an office in Mum and Dad's home and so did his wife. They would arrive at Mum and Dad's early in the morning and returned to their house late in the evening, every day. While the rest of us moved away to other towns and countries, Bode stayed at home; the 'Home Boy'. I never remember Bode being sick. He was always there and always would be as far as my mind could imagine, with his wife. So I thought until the day I received a call from my brother, Austine. Bode had collapsed and lost consciousness and he was receiving care in a hospital. I'm sure Austine described the situation accurately, but my mind chose what information to receive. I was sure it would be only a matter of one or two days and Bode would be back home. We prayed. From our different locations, all seven siblings raised desperate cries to God and we trusted that God would restore Bode's health. Below are some excerpts of our siblings' conversation, praying and in full hope that Bode would get well and be back home again.

- [17/05/2018, 08:59] Olubusola: We are praying. TOTAL RESTORATION
- [17/05/2018, 09:45] Olusolape: Divine restoration for him

- [17/05/2018, 10:07] Olusolape: The Lord will perfect it in Jesus name.
- [17/05/2018, 10:53] Jimi: The Lord will take over and restore Boda Bode to full health and vitality
- [17/05/2018, 11:11] OluFunke: **Please pray on**
- [17/05/2018, 11:12] OluFunke: Prelim results not nice
- [17/05/2018, 11:13] Austine: I have told God
- [17/05/2018, 11:22] Olufunmi: Hmmmmm, it is well. God we depend on you
- [17/05/2018, 14:04] OluFunke: **Please pray on.** We need God's intervention more than ever
- [17/05/2018, 14:09] OluFunke: For a miraculous healing and recovery
- [17/05/2018, 14:24] Olusolape: The Lord is on the throne
- [17/05/2018, 14:35] Austine: God is always faithful
- [17/05/2018, 14:41] Aanu Oyewo: We shall have a testimony in Jesus name
- [17/05/2018, 18:14] Austine: **Pls pray people**
- [17/05/2018, 18:15] Austine: And they said the situation is not looking good
- [17/05/2018, 18:17] Austine: I know I serve a God who can turn situation around
- [17/05/2018, 18:17] Austine: For good
- [17/05/2018, 18:17] Jimi: Amen!

All seven of us and our families prayed and hoped for his full recovery. We trusted in our prayer-answering God to restore Bode's health.

- [17/05/2018, 18:27] Austine: Thank you all for your prayers
- [17/05/2018, 18:29] Austine: Just got a call from the

Dr now that Brother Bode gave up

So, Bode never regained consciousness; he died in two days. I howled and wept myself sore. But as I looked back on the WhatsApp conversations I had with my siblings on the day he died and the day following, I realise that I made some choices based on the understanding of some of the ideas I propose in this book. I will share some of these messages leaving in a few bits by my siblings to give context to the conversation (all emphasis not in the original messages)

- [17/05/2018, 18:42] Olubusola Eshiet: My words are **frozen**!
- Bode died! Can my brother die like that? **Will God raise him? I'm not ready to let him go**. Just like that?
- [18/05/2018, 06:49] Olubusola Eshiet: In all, we thank God that He gave us ease of receiving the best possible care for Bode. Let us take comfort in that we could not have done anything more than we did to keep him. We prayed, we moved, God gave us open doors. To Him be glory.
- [18/05/2018, 11:11] Olubusola Eshiet: Please make room for a closed-door discussion with Bode's wife before or after the burial. Let her know that in practical terms that we will support her and that she and the children, will NOT be left to languish. Sorrow of loss should be separated from worry about the future.
- [18/05/2018, 11:19] Olubusola Eshiet: A perspective I'm working from now: Bode was a loan, a lovely one. We enjoyed him while the loan lasted. We knew it would end one day but as a loved loan, we wish it wouldn't. Let us thank God for flavouring

our lives with Bode. Thank God that he was so precious, he loved us so much and we loved him real much. The owner has claimed his loan. We can only be thankful that we were beneficiaries of this loan and for this long. This thought has helped me this morning.

- [18/05/2018, 11:25] Olubusola: Same feel. But it is real. I can't imagine it. But no need trying to imagine reality. I can only see him standing tall and giving me his warm embrace

- [18/05/2018, 13:56] Olubusola: [18/05, 11:29] Olusolape: We love you brother

- [18/05, 11:30] Olufunmi: Broda mi Bode, my Egbon, my handyman. Goodnight

- [18/05, 11:44] Aanu: Too soon boda m Bode. Haaaa.........

- [18/05, 11:53] Olubusola: Is it Bode true true, Bode Bodis Bod my Bode

- [18/05, 12:16] Olubusola Eshiet: The man who none of us can remember a hard moment with. The man who was always there for us. The man who I thought would be my attraction to Iloti when my mum and dad have gone to glory. To the man who loved us and our descendants to bits.

- We love you Bodes Bod.

- [18/05, 12:22] Jimi: Never complained, grumbled, nor demanded anything. Always fought for us; was our mouthpiece and advocate! My big brother and friend!!! Will miss you, Boda mi

REFLECTIONS ON MY EXPERIENCES

Mama

I expected she would die though I wished she never

would. We always said our goodbyes at each parting as though that would be the last. So, you can imagine that each visit was loaded with affectionate experiences, each giving their best to the other. It was not a surprise, we were prepared. This attitude minimised the pain; just as Alison, Eby and Vida expressed in earlier chapters.

While it may be practicable to sustain this attitude with our older relatives and friends, it may not be as easy with people we consider young and so we expect will live for much longer. But the question is how old is a person, really? This is probably the simplest of all the questions I have posed in this book; of course, a person is as old as they are, and their birth certificates are there to prove this. Tony Evans in his Reflections on the death of his wife, Lois Evans said:

We really don't know today who the old people are in the church because how old you are is not determined by your birthdate but by your death date. If you're fifty and only going to make it to sixty you're old. If you're fifty and go live to be a hundred you're still pretty young but since you don't know whether you're gonna make it to 50 or 100 you don't know who the old folks are here today. Many people think they're younger when they're older than they think because we don't know that time begins to dawn.[2]

If we think this way, we will be more affectionate towards each other every time and so be in a prepared position every time. What is more, our world will be a happier place to live in. Everyone gains whether we live, or we die.

Christine

I loved my friend and knew immediately that I had lost her but I was keen to help my surviving friend (her husband) to come to terms with the reality and to inform his office so he could focus on the next actions that would be required of him. I wanted to go to their house and see if the children were okay or to tell them 'aunty' is still here. I responded in that moment to a sense of responsibility to make things work that could work. But I grieved for a long time. I would look at pictures of Christine, or Christine and I, and feel awful. One picture is cemented on my mind though it is now about 20 years ago. At the first thought of her, I can see that picture clearly.

Ekemini

I will describe my relationship with Ekemini's as doting – as would be expected of a mother and son. My response was shock, and confusion. I walked through the grief for more than a year, but the pain gradually began to reduce until I found myself accepting very reluctantly that he was indeed gone for good.

Bode (the most recent)

To different degrees, I was frozen - numb. I am not known to lack words though I may not describe myself as talkative. I wasn't ready to let go.

I hoped that God would raise Bode. After all, we have many testimonies of dead raised to life in our times. (My brother, Austine refused to let them pack the corpse until he had prayed over the corpse for a restoration of life. He let go when life did not return to Bode.)

I gave thanks that in the short time available, we gave Bode the best care possible and we prayed the best we could. I advised my siblings to give thanks to God as I was doing for the temporary gift of Bode. I mentioned that I found this attitude helpful.

I accepted that it was real and Bode was dead, never to give me those warm embraces again in this life. There was instability in my feeling and communication as minutes later, I asked if it was true that Bode was dead.

My One Regret

I wish I had told him how much I loved him and that my love for him and his family was as strong as to make me travel to anywhere he would live even after Mum and Dad were gone. I didn't tell him how much I loved him. I did show it and I believe he knew it. To be fair to myself, it is not in our growing up culture to express our love and appreciation for one another in such a verbal way, we just showed by action. But hopefully, I'm doing more of adding those verbal expressions to those I still have with me.

I was going away on a strategic planning retreat which I was co-leading when Bode became ill and so during much of the conversation about his sickness until his death, I was either on my trip to the venue of the retreat or at the retreat. Many things at the retreat depended on my ability to function well. I could have asked for permission to return home and my colleague offered to release me if I wanted but I asked myself what good that would do. It wouldn't bring my brother back to life and I would have ruined the company's retreat. I thought I did my part of the retreat as well as I planned to and the feedback I received from my colleague affirmed this.

I still had the rest of the grief work to do but I think I healed faster than in previous bereavements. I had already started thinking deeply about writing this book by then so some of the ideas on coping with grief were helpful to me. Three months later, when it became possible for me to visit Mum, Dad, and Bode's family, I wasn't sure how I would manage. I shed some secret tears as I didn't want to unsettle the people, but I managed very well. However, I didn't go to his gravesite. I would some other time. Bode lives in my heart.

ॐ 6 ॐ

When I watch you leave
And I say those words of love and release
Though ever so reluctantly and with great pain
    in my heart
May I **stay on** strong in the love of Christ our
    Saviour
As you **fly off** safe into our Saviour's arms
- Olubusola Eshiet

*Every test that you have experienced is the kind that normally comes
to people. But God keeps his promise, and he will not allow you to be
tested beyond your power to remain firm; at the time you are put to
the test, he will give you the strength to endure it, and so provide you
with a way out. 1Corinthians 10:13 (GNT)*

6: VICTORIOUS IN LOSS

Everyone who lives long enough will face loss and will grieve the loss of dear ones. My daughter was only five years old when her friend mentioned earlier died but she says she can never forget. It was her first experience of death. It only takes half of a sentence about the incident and she remembers the name of her friend.

Using the preparation gained from the experience of others or our previous experiences is helpful. The aim of this chapter is to explore the possibility of taking charge of our grief instead of allowing it to just happen to us. How can we apply the preparation of mind to help us in times of grief?

WHAT YOU MAY EXPERIENCE WHEN GRIEF COMES

The knowledge of what we may expect when loss happens if applied in our situations of loss, should help us in how we navigate the grief process.

Will I be heartbroken?

This is to be expected unless you have agreed to learn from Smith Wigglesworth (see chapter 2) and Charles Finney (see chapter 3).

What may your experience of grief entail?

People talked about physical pains e.g. pains in the stomach, headaches, fever, smarting eyes, pain from additional pumping of the heart. Emotional experiences include: disorientation, fear of the future, fear of not being able to raise children, fear of dying of the same illness that led to their loved one's death, fear that their loved one didn't go to heaven or wondering where their loved one is now, fear of the future, etc. Lack of zest for life which could even include suicidal thoughts. People also experienced inability to function well in daily routines.

In addition, people say these pains and fears are more intense when they are alone, especially at night. It is helpful to remember that these pains can be controlled using some of the coping ways that were suggested earlier.

Can I experience the peace (comfort) that is beyond understanding and experience an immediate healing?

If you want this, going by the experiences of Finney and Wigglesworth above and if you believe them, it is possible. And did I hear you say: 'if God speaks to me the way he spoke to them?' You shouldn't have to wait for your own voice from heaven because we are encouraged to believe the prophets of God, are we not? 2 Chronicles 20:20 says: 'Believe in the Lord your God; so shall ye be established. Believe His prophets; so shall ye prosper.' (KJV)

I do believe them, AND I would like the experience! But I wonder, and I have talked this over with my husband, if it would have a sense of disloyalty to someone I have loved for all my life if I walk away from their corpse feeling happy for them and I step out and have life go on for me. I have an 'approach avoidance' syndrome here, I confess. I want it yet I do not want it. I believe it is possible and I have experienced it with temporary parting with friends and with my husband as I mentioned in the introduction.

Should I eat? Is it a lack of loyalty to my dead loved one if my appetite is as sharp as always?

Does the dead person need food? They don't but you need it; go for it. Your tasks haven't suddenly reduced neither has your body stopped needing energy to function. So, you should eat as much as you need to. Drink enough fluid also, as you can't get this wrong. Fluid is always good.

Should I talk about them, laugh or is it a sign of disloyalty, or even irreverence to the departed?

Talking about the dead loved one is helpful. People have felt like talking endlessly about their loved one who has just died. Talking about how they would do things, what they meant to you and how you miss them is normal. Someone said, 'I was so consumed by the desire to constantly talk about him and I had to caution myself not to speak to strangers about him.' If possible, at such times, you may find it beneficial to speak to a friend or family member. If there's no one available physically, it may be possible to call someone up on the phone.

A smile is always good and if you feel like laughing, why not? I think even those occasional spells of expressing joy are good during periods of deep sorrow. If you talk about the dead person as naturally as possible, there will be moments of laughter as well as tears.

Cry? Stop crying?

It is okay to cry. Even Jesus wept. God makes a note of

our tears and records them all in his book. It matters to God and he comforts us in our weeping.

> *You have collected all my tears in Your bottle. You have recorded each one in your book. Psalm 56:8 (ESV)*

> *He (the Lord) heals the brokenhearted and binds up their wounds. Psalm 147:3*

> *Blessed are those who mourn for they will be comforted. Matthew 5:3*

The Holy Spirit is the Comforter. He is always available to help us and to bring comfort. Be aware of this immeasurable source of help and receive it in your time of need.

Will I be lonely?

Highly likely, you'll miss the person who has died; you may even feel angry at them for leaving you. Also, people will soon return to their normal life and the string of visits will reduce – that is, if you had visits. In some cultures, people visit and spend nights with the bereaved. This can go on for weeks or even longer. People want to speak to you or visit you, they can't imagine why not. But you need to rest and sometimes you may not even feel like seeing anyone. At such times, you should gently but firmly excuse yourself and get the needed rest or solitude.

After John the Baptist was killed by Herod, Jesus went took some time off his daily schedule.

> *When Jesus heard what had happened, he withdrew by boat privately to a solitary place. Matthew 14:13*

On another occasion, Jesus left the multitudes behind and took his disciples to the Garden of Gethsemane. When they got there, he took the three disciples who were always with him at special event to go with him on this journey. At a point, Jesus went away on his own:

> *Then Jesus went with his disciples to a place called*
> *Gethsemane, and he said to them, "Sit here while*
> *I go over there and pray." He took Peter and the*
> *two sons of Zebedee along with him, and he began*
> *to be sorrowful and troubled. Then he said to*
> *them, "My soul is overwhelmed with sorrow to*
> *the point of death. Stay here and keep watch*
> *with me."*
> *Going a little farther, he fell with his face to the*
> *ground and prayed, Matt 26: 36-39.*

If Jesus, who was God himself, needed that time alone when he was in agony of heart, I imagine that anyone could have such moments when they want to be alone. If you allow the fear of offending people stop you from getting the rest your body needs or spending time on your own, you may fall ill. It's far better to say no to visits and calls when you need to and to take the time to rest as often as you need to. When you say 'no' to the visits, it may be good to give an idea of when you will be available, otherwise you may find yourself lonely and wishing people would visit you. At the same time, your friends not wanting to disturb you may choose not to visit or call you. And if you are the friend or neighbour who wants to help by visiting, calling on the phone, making meals, praying with, and offering other practical help, don't be offended if the bereaved can't accept all that you have to offer.

In writing the above, I am aware that in some societies,

e.g. today's British society, people stay away and don't visit or talk about the bereavement to the person who is bereaved. Death is treated a taboo, not to be mentioned, a very personal and private thing. I remember a friend from Northern Ireland who returned to her office in England from her father's funeral and her colleagues in the office didn't say a word to her. She wished that someone would acknowledge that she was grieving, give her a bouquet of flowers and say some tender words. But life just went on in the office as normal. She said: 'I do not like the way the English respond to death, no one said a word to me.'

It appears that whatever the culture, humans all grieve, and they could all do with some help. People need to say something, look the situation in the eye and acknowledge that the person is grieving. Another British friend said: 'In Britain, people speak about the dead in hushed tones. But it is important to laugh about them, smile about them.' Obviously, one of the reasons people don't say anything is the fear of saying the wrong things to the bereaved, a very real fear as many people do get it wrong.

A quick guide to what to say is just to say, 'I am sorry for your loss' and 'I am praying for you'. If you are not praying, please do not add the bit about prayer. In most cases, all that the person in grief needs from you is your presence. Rick Warren says, 'show up and shut up'[1] and he should know, having experienced the loss of a son. You should be a good listener and try to reflect what they say to you.

Dealing with loneliness: you can call people and let them know you are lonely. Get friends to accompany you on walks, to come over, to cook with you, eat with you, physical or by video calls. Ask for practical help, some people don't know what you need though they would love to help, they may not even know that you have needs.

Also remember God is always with you even when you

don't feel his presence. God will never leave you nor forsake you (Deuteronomy 31:6).

What about when people say the annoying and thoughtless things to me?

Be yourself even when people say to you those annoying, thoughtless things that they shouldn't say. Be in control. I heard of one such recently: 'He's gone to heaven ahead of you to welcome you when you arrive.' The bereaved said she wondered what the angels would be doing if her husband needed to leave that early to be able to receive her. That was no help at all.

No matter how much the word is put out there to not say such things, people will still say them to you because they are uninformed. But you can be prepared to hear them and to be unruffled when such comes. Let the knowledge that people may say such things to you serve as a protective measure against them having a devastating effect on you. If you are so prepared, you may be able to kindly let people know that such sayings do not help - not for your sake (you are well prepared for them) but for the sake of others that they would try to comfort in future. Preparation may not take away the sting of thoughtless comments but can cushion the effect of the comments.

Feeling of shame, and vulnerability; having a longing to hear the person's voice again

Some bereaved people have expressed feelings of shame and being particularly vulnerable. As a widow said:

I felt that I had been unclothed by his death. I felt vulnerable and dreaded going outside my house. I developed a phobia for the opposite sex, afraid that someone might want to take advantage of me.

Also, there could be an intense longing to hear the voice

of the departed just one more time. This is normal and people would resolve this in different ways. Someone said they played videos of the departed again and again and went back frequently to the text messages they shared to find consolation and to laugh at their jokes. Another person talked of calling the departed's phone to listen to his recorded voice message.

If the dead person was hard, disapproving, bullying, domineering, or even abusive

You may have a potpourri of feelings from relief that it is all over, to guilt at what could or could not have been said or done by you and or anger at what your dead loved one failed to do. It is not helpful to deify the dead one but to be real about the relationship, accept your faults, forgive yourself and the dead one for identified failings and accept the fact that you can't undo the past.

Dealing with Guilt

Even when the relationship was good, there may some-times be feelings of regrets at things you thought you could have done to make the relationship better or to even prevent the death of the loved one. But as mentioned above, you should absolve or forgive yourself of any real or perceived fail-ings. An example is the father who thought that his daughter may have lived if he visited her on the weekend that she died. He didn't make the visit for unavoidable reasons. He should tell himself that he couldn't possibly have made the visit and so free himself of the guilt.

Will I ever feel happy again?

Understandably, this is one question people who grieve must deal with. Closely linked to this for married people is the question 'will I remarry?' Interestingly, a young lady told me that she and her fiancée talked about 'the death thing' but continued by saying that they don't want to think about such things. Her words: 'who wants to think of sadness, remarriage etc?' But this does show that even before marrying, such thoughts cross some people's minds.

Some people who lost their spouses have said that the thought of remarrying came to their minds soon after the loss of their spouses – not the desire to remarry but thoughts of whether they would ever remarry. Someone expressed a fear of never meeting someone as special as their dead spouse.

Grief is an incalculable wound and anyone who has had a wound no matter how small knows the desire to have the wound healed so they can function properly again. But no matter how deep the wound of grief is, people who have known grief agree that there is always healing. How quickly healing will take place depends on many factors but the happy news is that there will be healing.

Knowing that healing will come and so will joy and love for life can help in times of grief. Psalm 30:5 says: weeping may stay for the night, but rejoicing comes in the morning. David Baroni, in the song: *Faithful God*[2], sings 'there has never been a night without a dawn'.

Psalm 30:11 gives the assurance that God turns our mourning into dancing; and Isaiah 60:20 says 'your days of sorrow will end'.

7

I may leave you here
You may leave me here
But we will meet again
If we remain true to Our Saviour
Have you met Him though?
The Saviour, Redeemer
He promised us a place
Where we'll all meet again
Oh, what joy!
- *Olubusola Eshiet*

Do not let your hearts be troubled. You believe in God; believe also in me. My Father's house has many rooms; if that were not so, would I have told you that I am going there to prepare a place for you? And if I go and prepare a place for you, I will come back and take you to be with me that you also may be where I am. John 14:1-3

7: FINISH STRONG

This has been a journey for me, and I have made many discoveries. One maybe not so grand but highly motivating discovery is this: the author is the first reader of her book. So, I will share my journey of writing the book but, first, I invite you to once again answer the questions that you did earlier and see if you can trace your own journey through the book. It does not matter if you finished reading the book in two hours, two weeks, or longer; you may have had a journey and maybe some of your answers have changed just a bit.

The questions aim to find out your readiness to talk about death and willingness to prepare your mind for possible death of loved ones of any age.

1. In what specific ways do you miss someone you love when you have to part from them for a relatively long time (e.g. travel, relocation, etc.)?
2. What things do you think you will miss about your loved ones if they should die before you do (please state relationships)?

3. What makes the relationships with your loved ones special to you?
4. What are your immediate thoughts/feelings on thinking they may die before you?
5. Do you talk to your loved ones about their death and your death?
6. Imagine you hear that they have died, how does this make you feel?
7. How will you cope with the grief of losing them?
8. What regrets would you have if they died suddenly?
9. Are there activities that you can engage in now that will make your loss more bearable, e.g. how to do things around the home, places to go, or general information?

While thinking of the contents of this last chapter, I had an experience which tested my readiness for news I never wanted to hear.

I reconnected by phone with my friend, Ijeoma, whose name appeared in earlier chapters, whom I hadn't communicated with in about four years. I asked the usual question I would ask a married friend after asking 'how are you?' In her case, I asked 'how is my brother, Ikay[1]?' as is customary of Nigerian believers when asking for the wellbeing of a friend's husband. I don't know what could have prepared me for her response if writing this book had not. 'Your brother died of cancer three years ago.' It seemed I would faint, and I had that just-been-kicked-in-the-stomach feeling. She added in the same moment, 'I recently remarried'. No doubt, the second piece of information brought me joy. My summary: 'Ikay has gone to heaven; God has helped Ijeoma through the grief and restored her'. I know it would have been crushing if I had to think that my friend was now living in grief and loneliness, however, I found that I was processing the joy separately from the sorrow. I went online looking for his pictures, found and read a newspaper article that reported his death, and I spent the rest of the evening a bit down. I woke up in the morning still sad about the death and glad that my friend found a life again and I continued with this chapter.

I wish I could say I was now prepared for expected departures to the extent that I walked away from my friend's news with a 'praise God - Ikay has gone to heaven and alleluia - Ijeoma has remarried.' That would have been a good end to report. I remembered all the advice on preparing for and dealing with grief, I told myself: 'physician, heal thyself.' But I had those agonising pangs of grief again. This made me remember that my friend Lesley said, 'nothing can fully prepare you to not have that person in your life anymore'. However, in addition to the help I received from the good news of Ijeoma's remarriage, the advice in this book has been helpful and the fact that I was writing this part of the book just then.

One more experience. As I was concluding this chapter and nursing my own grief at the news of my friend's husband who died three years ago, a friend called me to say her husband, Leo was grieving the loss of a dear friend. He was totally unprepared for the news. They were classmates and belonged to the same Christian group at university. After university education, they went their separate ways and didn't meet for more than thirty years. They had recently reconnected through social media and they communicated with one another regularly. Leo had been rather busy so had been away from group chats. It was shocking for him therefore to see the friend's death announcement on social media. He was devastated! He felt that he should have paid more attention to the relationship after they rediscovered each other. He was going to miss hearing his friend call him 'Leoboy'. Leo is over sixty, but he still cherished that nickname he acquired in his twenties. In fact, the departed friend was the only one who still called him that nearly forty years after they left university. Leo dedicated two days of a music program he anchors to the memory of this beloved friend. That was a good gesture but think about how much more celebratory the days would have been if he did this while she was still alive.

I was again reminded that we will all die and that we may not be able to avoid grieving. So, we should make preparation for parting with our loved ones a constant practice. It is a practice that brings only gain, no losses. When you relate to your loved one as if you know that they are borrowed *and* for a short period of time, your relationships will be sweeter, and your lives more enjoyable.

No matter how much you may be confronted with grief (some of us may have greater times of it than others do), you can live life well, with confidence and you can finish with joy.

ARE YOU READY?

When you answered the questions at the beginning of this chapter, did you feel any more prepared to talk about death, or even to face moments of grief than you did at the start of the book? Even so, there is another preparation that we all need to make: preparation to die. Many of the suggestions about how to prepare for the loss of loved ones also help us to prepare for our own death. Additionally, there is another part of the preparation that we need to make for our death to be ready for our transition.

I mentioned earlier that I look forward to going to heaven and meeting Jesus, my Saviour and Lord. The most likely way to get to heaven is to die. The Bible records only two people who have gone to heaven without dying: Enoch (Genesis 5:21) and Elijah (2 Kings 2:11-12). This is such a minority that it is easier for me to believe that I will die than to think that I will not. Although death is the end to life as we know it now, death is only a transition to a place of continuation of life forever. Even Enoch and Elijah changed location, they left the earthly existence to another realm of existence. Jesus said to his disciples then and those who are his disciples today:

> *Do not let your hearts be troubled. You believe in*
> *God; believe also in me. My Father's house has*
> *many rooms; if that were not so, would I have*
> *told you that I am going there to prepare a place*
> *for you? And if I go and prepare a place for you, I*
> *will come back and take you to be with me that*
> *you also may be where I am. John 14:1-3*

It is to that heavenly city that I look forward when I sing the songs about heaven. It is a place of life with God. Just as was said of Ravi Zacharias, I also know that my death bed will be a 'launching pad'; a point of release into my eternal home. This assurance doesn't come because I am good, or I do many good things. No one can please God and so earns a place in heaven. It is the gift of God.

> *For it is by grace you have been saved, through faith*
> *—and this is not from yourselves, it is the gift of*
> *God—not by works, so that no one can boast.*
> *Ephesians 2: 8-9*

My assurance that I will go to heaven comes from believing in the Lord Jesus Christ and by receiving him as my Lord and Saviour. This is the belief that makes death a thing to look forward to instead of being afraid of it.

Do you also feel ready to die if your time comes now? Or

are you afraid of what lies on the other side of death? Are you sure you will go to heaven and spend eternity with God who loves you and looks forward to spending eternity with you when you die? Just as you had a physical birth when you were born into this world, you can have a spiritual birth if you want to by receiving Jesus Christ into your heart to be your Saviour and Lord. When you receive spiritual birth, you become Jesus' disciple and so, one of those for whom He is preparing a place. This gives you the assurance of a place in heaven and so you can be confident to meet God when you die.

If you are not sure you are ready to meet God when you die and you would like to be, I invite you to pray the following prayer.

Prayer:

Lord Jesus, I believe You died and rose again from the dead to save me from my sins. I am sorry for living to please myself and I ask you to forgive me from my sins. Would you please come into my heart and be Lord of all that I think, do and say now and always? Thank you for forgiving me and for coming to live in my heart. Amen

If you have just prayed the above, the following verses from the Bible will help you to know that you are forgiven and accepted by God.

> *If you declare with your mouth, "Jesus is Lord," and believe in your heart that God raised him from the dead, you will be saved. For it is with your heart that you believe and are justified, and it is with your mouth that you profess your faith and are saved. Romans 10:9-10*

Yet to all who did receive him, to those who believed in his name, he gave the right to become children of God. John 1:12

There are many more such verses in the Bible. In addition, you should find a church that preaches salvation through Jesus Christ and let someone know you recently made this decision and they can help you understand more about your journey here until you go to heaven.

AFTERWORD

As I was reading through the last draft of this book, it struck me that I had missed a little detail: I didn't mention my grandfather when writing about my experiences of bereavement. So, I thought I would just include the words 'my grandfather' at an appropriate point in the book. So, I did. But as I scrolled through the draft 'one final time' before sending it off for publishing, all that I had been reading about the care of children when there is bereavement in the family and about ungrieved bereavement came to the fore. I began to feel very emotional. Things seemed to start coming together.

You may remember reading earlier that my first mum was my grandmother.

When I was a child, my grandfather (dad) was killed in a car accident less than an hour after he left home on an errand. As I write this, I hear in my head – as I always do when I remember this event - my grandmother saying to her co-wife who was preparing my grandfather's breakfast (in my native dialect, Ijebu but translated) 'Mama ..... don't make the cereal anymore, the person you're making it for is dead!'

For years, I thought of my grandfather's death. I felt he

left too early. Whenever I mentioned him to Emmanuel, I still tended to experience pain. But today I realised that I had never dealt with that grief. The fact that I had unfinished grief work was so hidden that I didn't even remember my grandfather while I was writing the book. It has been a tearful morning for me. Also, I cry as I realise that the root of my fear of loss of loved ones, especially about Emmanuel not returning from trips may have been directly connected to having lost my grandfather in such circumstances.

My favourite scripture passage when I'm preparing to write or teach is: 1 Timothy 2:6. I first learnt and loved it in the King James Version, and it says 'The husbandman that laboureth must be first partaker of the fruits.' The NIV says, 'The hardworking farmer should be the first to receive a share of the crops.'

I always hoped to be the first to reap the benefit of what I prepare to share with others, whether as a validation of my daily living, an assurance of his love or guidance or a gentle warning from God to me. So, I'm thankful to God for his extraordinary kindness, gentleness and compassion in showing me something so important – the root of my fear – and for his redemptive work of delivering me from the fear of loss.

AUTHOR'S NOTE

Help Spread the Word!

Share a link to the book and mention it on social media.

Write a review on your blog, on a bookseller site, or on Facebook, anywhere you'd like.

Talk about the ideas in the book with your family, colleagues, pastor, church, city groups, boss, staff, your students, parents, friends and neighbours.

We invite you to share your response to this book by emailing:

info@optimalpathconsulting.co.uk

HELPFUL RESOURCES

Helpful Resources

1.   **https://www.beliefnet.com/love-family/life-events/how-should-christians-approach-the-death-of-a-loved-one.aspx**

2. **Living well in the end times - http://www.oxford. anglican.org/wp-content/uploads/2013/01/OD705-Living-well-book.pdf**

3. **https://www.artofdyingwell.org/** The Centre for the Art of Dying Well at St Mary's University. Rethinking the art of accompaniment at the end of life. Public engagement, policy, research - death, dying and bereavement.

4. **https://xerte.cardiff.ac.uk/play_5767#page1** – A "Christian perspective on death and dying" toolkit

5.   **https://www.dyingmatters.org/overview/ resources** - Since the Dying Matters Coalition was set up in 2009, they've created a wide range of resources to help people start conversations about dying, death and bereavement.

6. **https://www.ageuk.org.uk/information-advice/**

Legal & Estate Planning

Many people choose to, and should, use an attorney. However, if you can't or just won't, almost everyone agrees that *something is better than nothing*.

Look out for articles, blogs and guidance notes on Wills, Living Trusts etc. Below are samples:

1.   **https://www.ageuk.org.uk/globalassets/age-uk/ documents/information- guides/ageukig31_wills_and_estate_planning_inf.pdf**

2.   **https://www.which.co.uk/money/wills-and- probate/passing-on-your-money/will-trusts-and- lifetime-trusts-aqmf66w4nu5w**

3. Wills and Trusts Kit for Dummies by Aaron Larson

End-of-Life Planning

Knowing what someone wants or sharing what 'quality of life means to you is priceless and have been some of the most meaningful conversations of my life.

1. Talk About (talking about) It: *Death Over Dinner* offers a free guide and invitation advice. *The Conversation Project* has tons of free resources. ***The Art of Dying Well: A Practical Guide to a Good End of Life*** by Katy Butler helps us learn and prepare.

2.   **https://www.dyingmatters.org/ overview/resources**

Digital Accounts & Passwords

Don't lose important things and save yourself (and eventually others) dozens of hours trying to get online access.

Apps like *LastPass* (the free version) can be used to manage digital accounts, some friends prefer **Dashlane**. Either one (or others) allow you to save, store and share your details.

Money & Personal Finance

1. **https://www.moneysavingexpert.com/** provides good guidance on money matters

2. ***Your Money or Your Life: 9 Steps to Transforming Your Relationship with Money and Achieving Financial Independence*** by Vicki Robin and Joe Dominguez.

3. **The Index Card: Why Personal Finance Doesn't Have to Be Complicated.** by Helaine Olen and Harrold Pollack.

Insurance

Yes, I know insurance is hard to buy and you hope you won't need. However, it is super helpful for many people, and if/when you ever do need it, you're *really* going to appreciate having it.

If you can't get life (or disability) insurance through your work, you can shop and buy online.

Some companies offer term life insurance online, it does not require a medical examination and the application process is easy You can also compare prices on sites like *Policy Genius* (life, disability and other types of policies).

Dying, Grief & Loss

1. *The Art of Dying Well: A Practical Guide to a Good End of Life*

2. ***Modern Loss: Candid Conversation About Grief. Beginners Welcome*** by Rebecca Soffer and Gabrielle Birkner.

3. ***It's OK That You're Not OK: Meeting Grief and Loss in a Culture That Doesn't Understand***

NOTES

PROLOGUE: GOD FORBID!

1. A famous proverb

PROLOGUE

1. Revd Canon Yvonne Richmond Tulloch. Webinar: The Bereavement Friendly Church, www.lossandhope.org

CHAPTER 1

1. Colin Murray Parkes. Oxford Essential Quotations

FEAR OF LOSS

1. Priscilla Shirer : Fear Not https://www.youtube.com/watch?v=FeLoU9rbZXc
2. Interview at 'Desperate for Jesus Conference 2020' https://www.youtube.com/watch?v=Nho8w9XSMCc
3. Priscilla Shirer. Identity in Christ https://www.youtube.com/watch?v=klkEKMTe3OY
4. Ravi Zacharias' Memorial service https://www.bing.com/videos/search?q=ravi+zacharias+memorial+service&view=detail&mid=9364653471ECAB3BACF89364653471ECAB3BACF8&FORM=VIRE

2: MOURNING MY WAY

1. Eugene Nida and Johannes P. Louw, *Greek-English Lexicon of the New Testament Based on Semantic Domains* (United Bible Societies, 1996).
2. Granger Westburg, *Good Grief*, 50th Anniversary Edition, Augsburg Fortress Press.
3. Wes Richards, *Hope and a Future* (Oxford, UK: Monarch Books), 95-96
4. Wes Richards p 96

5. Taken from Instantly a Widow by Ruth Sissom ©1990. Used by permission of Our Daily Bread Publishers, Box 3566, Grand Rapids, MI 49501. All rights reserved. Pg 3
6. Sissom pg 4
7. Sissom pp 19-20
8. Ravi Zacharias' Memorial Service https://www.bing.com/videos/search?q=ravi+zacharias+memorial+service&view=detail&mid=9364653471ECAB3BACF89364653471ECAB3BACF8&FORM=VIRE
9. Derek Prince Hope Beyond Grief (UK: Derek Prince Ministry – International, 2018), 39-43
10. Taken from Licking Honey Off a Thorn by Susan Lenzkes ©2002. Used by permission of Our Daily Bread Publishers, Box 3566, Grand Rapids, MI 49501. All rights reserved. Pg 15
11. Smith Wigglesworth, Faith that Prevails, 1938.

CHAPTER 3

1. Famous proverb I first learnt in my first language as: Ogun àgbọtẹ̀lẹ̀ kìi pa arọ

3: CHOICES

1. Also referred to as City Group or Connect Group – smaller groups where church members meet to have closer relationships with one another than they could during big Sunday meetings.
2. Charles G. Finney, An Autobiography.

4: PREPARING TO LET GO

1. Taken from God of Surprise by Willian Crowder c 2020. Used by permission of Our Daily Bread Publishers, Box 3566, Grand Rapids, MI: 49501 p. 26. All rights reserved.
2. God of Surprise, p 24
3. https://hellopoetry.com/poem/409553/love-me-before-i-die/
4. https://steemit.com/poem/@mrxplicit/poem-do-it-now-instead
5. Lois Evans and Friends, Seasons of a Woman's Life, https://www.youtube.com/watch?v=85HWoid3Qn4

5: MY FELLOWSHIP WITH BEREAVEMENT

1. https://internetpoem.com/ann-taylor/my-mother-poem/
2. Tony Evans, https://www.youtube.com/watch?v=QaoquYA9pNU

6: VICTORIOUS IN LOSS

1. https://www.oneplace.com/devotionals/daily-hope-with-rick-warren/you-cant-talk-people-out-of-their-pain-daily-hope-with-rick-warren-september-30-2020-11833362.html
2. David Baroni *Faithful God https://www.youtube.com/watch?v=eYiH-wW4_X9Q*

7: FINISH STRONG

1. Growing up as a Christian in Nigeria, we called each other 'brother' and 'sister' and we played the part. We considered one another as siblings, and Jesus Christ the first born in our family. The relationship was considered as close as any sibling relationship. I still feel the same way about believers that I meet regardless of race.

Printed in Great Britain
by Amazon